A JOURNEY TO
HAPPINESS

Discovering Well-Being through Tourism

ROBERTICO CROES, PH.D.

ARCHWAY
PUBLISHING

Archway Publishing books may be ordered through booksellers or by contacting:

Archway Publishing
1663 Liberty Drive
Bloomington, IN 47403
www.archwaypublishing.com
844-669-3957

ISBN: 978-1-6657-6590-9 (sc)
ISBN: 978-1-6657-6592-3 (hc)
ISBN: 978-1-6657-6591-6 (e)

Library of Congress Control Number: 2024919273

Print information available on the last page.

Archway Publishing rev. date: 10/02/2024

A destination that is not good for Residents is not good for Tourists (SDG11)

To my beloved late sister Mayrin,
whose absence weighs heavily on my heart.

A book by
Dr. Robertico Croes

Preface

THIS BOOK UNFOLDS THE TALE THAT BEGAN WITH MY JOURNEY TO Guayaquil, Ecuador, in 2007. Immersed in a project to maximize tourism's benefits for the local populace, I plunged into the intricacies of tourism development in a developing nation. Initially, I held firm to the belief that tracking tourist numbers and revenue alone would ensure substantial resident benefits. However, a transformative experience in late 20th-century Aruba shattered this conviction. Witnessing how tourism could revitalize an entire nation and elevate its living standards, I naively believed that jobs and income alone could suffice for happiness. Yet, the harsh reality of losing my career forced me to confront the fallacy of my assumptions. It became clear that residents sought more than just economic gains.

In Guayaquil, I pursued a more holistic approach to tourism development. Beyond creating jobs and boosting income, I recognized the imperative of enhancing residents' well-being, distinct from communal well-being. Disparity, limited opportunities, and barriers to seizing them could sour the purported benefits for specific individuals within the community. Through numerous visits to Guayaquil, this disparity became increasingly apparent, fueling my quest for the elusive equilibrium between tourism and genuine well-being.

I begin this book by paraphrasing the World Tourism Organization's perspective on SDG 11, Sustainable Cities and Communities. Instead of focusing solely on cities, I use the term "destinations" to encompass the broader tourism scope, including rural, beach, and mountain areas. Tourism and destinations share a symbiotic relationship, significantly influencing each other. Economically, destinations rely on tourism as a crucial revenue source, while tourism flourishes due to the appeal of diverse destinations. Culturally, tourism facilitates customs exchange, but destinations must balance preservation with visitor demands.

Environmentally, tourism can support conservation and strain resources, highlighting the need for sustainable practices.

However, this book transcends the mere balancing act of the symbiotic relationship between tourism and destinations. Unlike Jan H. de Kadt's "Tourism Passport to Development," published in 1979, which primarily served as a register for growth and social change, this work takes a different trajectory. Here, the focus pivots towards embracing well-being as the paramount objective of development. This entails a departure from the narrow confines of economic indicators to a more holistic evaluation encompassing the breadth of opportunities and freedoms conducive to meaningful experiences and achievements. The book is about human experience captured by assessing life and opportunities, including the freedom to achieve doings and beings.

This book has been an enriching odyssey, seamlessly weaving together research and personal exploration. Immersed in the tapestry of my own research and travels, I have unearthed the profound impact tourism wields on our mental and emotional landscapes and the dynamics it unfurls in local communities. This book has been an enriching journey, artfully blending research and personal experiences. Through my studies and travels, I've discovered the profound effects of tourism on our mental and emotional well-being and its transformative role in local communities. The book also answers Bruno Frey's call for inclusivity in happiness studies, highlighting the importance of considering both tourists and residents to fully understand tourism's significant impact on broader happiness literature.[1]

Digging deeper into the nexus of well-being and tourism, I have confronted the hurdles and possibilities confronting those who call destinations home. This introspection has sparked a reevaluation of my stance on

---

[1] Bruno S. Frey, 2020. "**What are the opportunities for future happiness research?**," International Review of Economics, Springer; Happiness Economics and Interpersonal Relations (HEIRS), vol. 67(1), pages 5-12, March.

sustainable travel and responsible tourism, prompting a shift in my journeying practices.

In essence, this endeavor has been a voyage of enlightenment, broadening my horizons and sharpening my focus on what matters in the pursuit of happiness — for myself and those I hold dear. As I offer these revelations, I extend heartfelt gratitude to my students for their inspiration, my colleagues' support, and my copy editor's invaluable contribution to refining this narrative into a precise, concise, and compelling tale.

Orlando, June 2024.

Foreword

TOURISM IS A MAJOR SOCIO-ECONOMIC FORCE GLOBALLY, IMPACTING everyone whether directly involved in the industry or not. Its activities bring both benefits and challenges to our communities. Tourism development plays a crucial role in enhancing the well-being of communities. Tourism development boosts local economies through job creation and business opportunities, thus it can lead to improved living standards. Enhanced amenities, such as parks, recreational facilities, and cultural and heritage attractions, contribute to the quality of life for residents. However, it is important to manage tourism sustainably to prevent issues like overcrowding, overuse of resources, environmental degradation, and increased living costs, which individually or in some combination can negatively impact community well-being. Balancing tourism growth with the preservation of local identity, culture, and environment is essential for ensuring long-term benefits to the well-being of both residents and visitors. The issue lies not in tourism itself, but in poor planning. A place that is great to live in can also be an attractive destination for visitors.

Destinations strive to remain competitive and sustainable by preserving natural and cultural resources, ensuring the well-being of residents, and providing satisfying experiences for visitors. The primary strategic goal for any destination is to mitigate the negative impacts of tourism while enhancing its positive effects. By balancing demand and supply, destinations can offer quality services and memorable experiences, support sustainable tourism development, and promote the well-being of stakeholders. Professor Robertico Croes' book, "A Journey to Happiness: Discovering Well-being through Tourism," provides a novel viewpoint and personal research journey on how tourism affects the quality of life in destination communities, leveraging his extensive research in various locations. This book delves into the connection between tourism development and well-being, using empirical evidence and examples from small microstates and developing countries. It examines the theoretical foundations of well-being and identifies its determinants.

Professor Croes skillfully discusses the relevant concepts of well-being, integrating both the economic and non-economic values of tourism activities. He explores how tourism development may or may not enhance the well-being of individuals, both as tourists and as residents. Through his Popperian approach to science, Croes challenges tourism researchers and practitioners to reassess their assumptions, uncover errors, and adapt new, evidence-based theories and practices. He emphasizes that "a destination that is not good for residents is not good for tourists," highlighting the need for continual refinement of strategies to ensure adaptability and responsiveness.

The book's message is clear. The complex, evolving nature of tourism requires constant attention. The link between tourism development and well-being is transformative and dynamic, necessitating careful planning, management, and monitoring to foster sustainable growth and community well-being.

Muzaffer Uysal, Ph.D.
Carney Family Endowed Professor
University of Massachusetts, Amherst, USA

Contents

Introduction

WHEN WE CONTEMPLATE TOURISM, WE OFTEN ENVISION A JOURNEY to a different destination with the aim of finding happiness. It is a quest to rejuvenate ourselves, gain fresh insights, and enrich our lives. Conversely, the residents who extend their warm welcome to tourists often believe that interacting with visitors brings enrichment to their own lives. Tourism has the potential to generate employment opportunities and offer a unique perspective on life. It is a mutual exchange of positivity and enriching experiences. But amidst all the optimism, one crucial question looms: Does tourism drive happiness and enhance overall well-being for both parties?

Is traveling to new places and experiencing diverse cultures a reliable path to personal happiness? Does it result in a lasting sense of well-being or just a fleeting moment of joy? Moreover, how does tourism impact the communities that open their doors to travelers? Does it bring sustainable economic benefits and improve the quality of life for the residents? Exploring these questions allows us to delve deeper into the complex relationship between tourism, happiness, and overall well-being. This book delves deeply into residents' well-being, shedding light on the interconnectedness between happiness, well-being, and the quality of life within communities touched by tourism.

Tourism involves individuals traveling to a destination outside their usual environment for under a year, driven by purposes like business or leisure, excluding employment in the visited country. The influx of international tourists significantly boosts a destination's economic development through foreign exchange earnings, job creation, and infrastructure enhancement. The economic impact of tourism includes direct effects on sales, employment, tax revenues, and income, as well as indirect impacts on prices, quality, and quantity of goods and services. Induced effects result in shifts in household spending from additional income from tourist expenditures. Additionally, tourism plays crucial roles in capital accumulation, poverty alleviation, and social welfare improvement. The sector's efficiency and productivity contribute to reducing costs, improving performance, and maintaining competitiveness.

Lastly, a country's tourism industry interacts with external economic factors in the global context, with tourism demand being sensitive to exchange rates and global economic conditions. Embarking on my academic journey in 2002 marked the genesis of a passionate dedication to the Rosen College of Hospitality Management, an essential pillar of the University of Central Florida in vibrant Orlando. Before my academic pursuits, I played pivotal roles in Aruba for an enriching fourteen years, assuming the responsibilities of elected offices such as Minister of Tourism, Economic Affairs, and Finance. This distinctive period not only charted the course of my professional trajectory but also bestowed upon me a wealth of invaluable insights at the crossroads of governance and the dynamic realm of hospitality and tourism.

Endowed with the opportunity to traverse the globe extensively, I immersed myself in the practical dimensions of tourism, systematically unraveling its dynamic nuances. My odyssey took me to diverse corners of the world, weaving through the tapestry of Latin America, Europe, Africa, and the Pacific. In these immersive explorations, I actively engaged in the hands-on facets of tourism, conducting systematic research to unveil the intricate layers of this vibrant field.

As my journey in sharing expertise unfolded across diverse global landscapes, the multifaceted nature of tourism's impact on happiness and well-being became increasingly apparent. Beyond the geographical expanse of over 25 countries, where my lectures and research presentations navigated the intricacies of tourism demand analysis, economic impacts, and sustainable practices, a deeper exploration emerged. This exploration extended beyond the boardrooms and academic arenas to the heart of communities, particularly in small islands and developing nations.

In the tapestry of my experiences, the threads of tourism development strategies for poverty alleviation and inclusive growth wove a narrative that transcended the conventional boundaries of academic inquiry. The pivotal question that emerged from these insights was whether tourism could transcend its economic dimensions to become a catalyst for happiness and well-being. This query opened a gateway to a two-decade-long exploration examining the relationship between travel and personal happiness and the intricate interplay with community impact.

Through this extensive voyage, a nuanced understanding crystallized: Travel, while reliably contributing to personal happiness, is a subjective journey shaped by individual preferences and experiences. The symbiotic relationship between tourism and economic benefits and cultural enrichment for host communities revealed both promises and perils. Economic advantages and cultural exchange must be managed precisely to ensure sustainability and safeguard the authentic local way of life.

The complex web linking tourism, happiness, and overall well-being demands ongoing scrutiny and consideration. As I reflect on the evolving dynamics of this relationship, the call for a holistic understanding becomes more resounding. The diverse factors in different destinations and circumstances underscore the need for a comprehensive approach that acknowledges the intricate tapestry woven by the threads of travel, happiness, and community impact.

My research in this area has evolved through conversations with my University of Central Florida students. As a social scientist who is deeply concerned about equity, inclusiveness, and democracy, I have applied these principles throughout my research journey, mainly focusing on the concept of vulnerability and its impact on individuals and regions. This exploration has led me to ponder a fundamental question: Can tourism contribute to the progress and happiness of vulnerable people and regions? This question has shaped my research focus, particularly on residents in small islands and developing countries. It is both an honor and a challenge to contribute to the discourse on a longstanding and debated topic. The privilege lies in the opportunity to share a personal perspective, while the challenge stems from the modest resolution of the issues at hand. I aspire to bring something valuable to the discussion.

The Pivotal Question

In my current research, I am investigating a significant and relevant question of profound importance. Not only can it provide answers, but it also has the potential to impact society substantially. To approach this question comprehensively, I am adopting a multidisciplinary perspective and employing various methods and arguments. Initially, I am delving into the broader ontological question of whether human behavior is solely determined by rationality and self-interest or whether more intricate factors are at play. By understanding whether individuals are motivated exclusively by self-interest or if other factors influence their behavior, we can derive valuable insights into how to assist vulnerable individuals.

Furthermore, I am delving into the impact of emotions like empathy and compassion in assisting those who are vulnerable. Acknowledging the pivotal role of empathy and compassion in interactions with vulnerable populations, I am exploring the emotional dynamics that play a significant role in this context and examining effective ways to integrate them into my research. Empathy involves understanding and sharing the feelings of others, such as their pain or distress, while compassion directs our actions toward addressing the emotions of others. To illustrate, empathy allows us to experience distress upon witnessing the struggles of a poor or disadvantaged child or a person with disabilities. In contrast, compassion inspires us to take action and extend assistance to the less fortunate, demonstrating our recognition of their challenges and our desire to help.[2] In essence, my research endeavors to unravel the complexity of human behavior and explore how this understanding can be harnessed to assist vulnerable individuals in their journey toward empowerment and happiness.

At the outset of my research, my primary focus revolved around examining the potential of tourism development in aiding small islands. Due to their limited size, these islands often face vulnerabilities and limited opportunities. By focusing on Caribbean islands, I sought to investigate how the expansion of tourism initiatives could provide them with increased prospects for growth. In doing so, I considered various factors, such as the unique characteristics of each island and the economic constraints they faced. Given my connection to the Caribbean and Latin American regions, having roots in Aruba, and being affiliated with the University of Central Florida for over two decades, I felt a deep drive to explore how travel and tourism could contribute to these areas' overall well-being and development. I published a book about constrained economies and another one about poverty reduction.[3]

Driven by a desire for broader insights and a comprehensive understanding, I gradually expanded my research to include other regional countries.

---

[2] Chierchia, G. and Singer, T. (2017). The Neuroscience of Compassion and Empathy and Their Link to Prosocial Motivation and Behavior, Chapter 20. In Jean-Claude Dreher and Léon Tremblay (eds.), *Decision Neuroscience*, Academic Press, Pages 247-257, ISBN 9780128053089, https://doi.org/10.1016/B978-0-12-805308-9.00020-8.
[3] Croes, R. (2023). *Small Island and small destination tourism. Overcoming the smallness barrier for economic growth and tourism competitiveness.* Apple Academic Press: Waretown, NJ, USA. Croes, R. & Rivera, M. (2016). *Poverty Alleviation through Tourism Development: A Comprehensive and Integrated Approach.* Apple Academic Press: Waretown, NJ, USA.

Mexico, Costa Rica, Nicaragua, Ecuador, Colombia, and Brazil became integral to my investigation, with each country providing unique perspectives and contexts. Subsequently, my curiosity grew to incorporate other islands, such as Malta in the Mediterranean, other developing countries like Malaysia, and transition economies like Poland.

The overarching goal of my research was to uncover specific ways in which tourism could positively impact individuals, destinations, and regions. I aimed to identify strategies that could help vulnerable communities overcome their challenges or, at the very least, mitigate the adverse effects of their vulnerability. By exploring the potential of tourism as a catalyst for progress and resilience, I endeavored to shed light on how these industries could serve as vehicles for inclusive growth and sustainable development.

A Popperian Approach

In the subsequent chapters, I will delve into the intricacies of my research, offering a closer examination of the specific approaches and findings that emerged during my investigation. At the heart of my research, a fundamental question arose as the central focus: Is it pertinent to explore the impact of tourism on vulnerable regions? Moreover, I contemplated who stood to benefit from the answers I sought and how my findings could be effectively applied to drive positive change. Recognizing the significance of these inquiries, they played a pivotal role in shaping the trajectory and methodology of my research.

To understand the topic comprehensively, it was essential to approach it from various perspectives. One notable approach involved adopting a doctor's perspective, employing a deductive reasoning process to analyze information and unravel the intricacies inherent in the question. Using this method, I aimed to discern whether individuals are primarily driven by rationality and self-interest or if their behavior encompasses more nuanced aspects. My inquiry through my writings adheres to the method suggested by Karl Popper.[4] He asserts that (imperfect) observations of the world are the basis of all sciences and that the scientific method rests on inferring general laws from these observations, supported by further (critical) testing (falsifying hypothesis).

According to Popper, each scientific theory is a conjecture or hypothesis harboring flaws. While temporarily escaping empirical testing, these flaws are destined to be exposed, leading to the theory being "falsified" by experience. In Popper's view, the progress of science unfolds through an iterative cycle of formulating assumptions, uncovering errors, facing denial, and subsequently proposing new assumptions.

Consider a prevalent hypothesis: "Increasing tourist arrivals always leads to positive economic benefits for a destination." Applying Popper's falsifiability criterion, we can subject this hypothesis to empirical scrutiny. A study is conducted on a popular tourist destination that has experienced a substantial increase in tourist arrivals over the past decade. The theory predicts unequivocally positive economic outcomes. However, the research reveals that the local economy has yet to experience the expected growth, and specific sectors, such as small local businesses, have faced challenges.

In this scenario, Popper's philosophy comes into play. The hypothesis, rather than being confirmed, is falsified by the empirical evidence. This doesn't negate the possibility that increasing tourist arrivals can have

---

[4] Karl Popper, a notable philosopher of science, is renowned for propounding the theory of falsification, a conceptual framework that demarcates scientific from non-scientific theories. This distinctive proposition revolves around scientific theories' inherent potential falsifiers, setting them apart from non-scientific counterparts. Popper posited that a hallmark of scientific legitimacy lies in the testability and refutability of a theory. According to Popper, the crux of scientific inquiry lies in the ability to subject theories to empirical scrutiny and, crucially, to the possibility of falsification. In Popper's view, scientific theories should be formulated to allow for the articulation of specific conditions or observations that, if found to be untrue or inconsistent, could refute the theory. This emphasis on falsifiability is a robust criterion for distinguishing scientific endeavors from non-scientific ones.

positive economic impacts, but it highlights the importance of recognizing conditions under which the hypothesis may not hold. As a result, the process continues after falsifying the initial hypothesis. Instead, it prompts the formulation of a new assumption that may better encapsulate the complex dynamics at play. For instance, the revised hypothesis could be: "The economic benefits of increasing tourist arrivals depend on effective destination management strategies that prioritize local businesses and community well-being."

This iterative process aligns with Popper's philosophy, continually emphasizing the need to refine theories based on empirical evidence. In the context of tourism, it encourages a more nuanced understanding of the relationship between tourist arrivals and economic outcomes, fostering adaptability and responsiveness to the industry's evolving nature.[5] Popperian logic in the context of tourism means that a deductive process between theory and evidence is never aimed at generating certainty but at gradually increasing our understanding of the tourist phenomena under study.

Furthermore, I recognized that vulnerability is a multifaceted concept and acknowledged the need to consider the diverse factors contributing to it. This involved exploring the structural, economic, and social dynamics that underpin vulnerability in various regions. By delving into these complexities, I aimed to uncover the underlying causes and identify strategies that could mitigate the adverse effects of vulnerability, particularly within the context of tourism. In my research, I also placed a significant emphasis on the application of my findings. It was not enough to generate knowledge; this knowledge needed to be translated into actionable insights. I sought to bridge the gap between theory and practice, considering how my research outcomes could be effectively implemented to drive positive change in vulnerable regions. This required collaboration

---

[5] See, for example, Ritchie, J. B., Sheehan, L. R. & Timur, S. (2008). Tourism Sciences or Tourism Studies? Implications for the Design and Content of Tourism Programming. *Téoros*, 27(1), 33–41. https://doi.org/10.7202/1070895ar.

with stakeholders, policymakers, and local communities to ensure the findings resonated with their needs and aspirations.

By considering a range of perspectives, I gained a more comprehensive understanding of the central question and effectively structured it to produce insightful and actionable answers. The aim was not merely to provide theoretical insights but also to generate practical outcomes that would make a tangible difference in the lives of individuals and communities. Thus, throughout my research, I focused on exploring the interplay between tourism development and well-being, recognizing their significance in shaping the trajectory of vulnerable regions.

Tourism Development and Well-being

From the early stages of my investigation, tourism development and well-being concepts took center stage. These constructs are inherently complex, encompassing a wide range of dimensions and interpretations. Tourism development pertains to the growth and enhancement of tourism activities within a region. It encompasses aspects such as infrastructure development, policy formulation, stakeholder engagement, and tourism's overall economic, social, and environmental impacts. Understanding the intricacies of tourism development requires a nuanced examination of these interrelated factors, recognizing that each region presents unique challenges and opportunities.

On the other hand, well-being encompasses a broader spectrum of dimensions, encompassing physical, psychological, social, and economic aspects of individuals' lives. It goes beyond material wealth and considers health, happiness, quality of life, and overall satisfaction. Unraveling the complexities of well-being requires a comprehensive approach, considering both subjective experiences and objective indicators.

Throughout my research, I examined the definitions, theories, and empirical studies surrounding tourism development and well-being. By engaging with existing scholarship, I sought to build upon the existing knowledge base and contribute new insights to the field. I explored various methodologies, including qualitative and quantitative approaches, to capture the multifaceted nature of these constructs and obtain a comprehensive understanding of their dynamics.

Moreover, I recognized that the relationship between tourism development and well-being is more fluid. While tourism has the potential to positively impact well-being by creating employment opportunities, fostering cultural exchange, and promoting economic growth, it can also present challenges and potential negative consequences, such as environmental degradation, social inequality, and cultural erosion. Understanding these intricate dynamics was vital in formulating strategies and recommendations to maximize the positive impacts while mitigating the potential drawbacks.

The chapters presented herein culminate my extensive research and collaboration with fellow scholars. This book is crafted to disseminate my research findings, with the hope that the information concerning tourism and well-being will contribute to the formulation and assessment of policies geared towards improving the well-being of destination residents and fostering evidence-based decision-making.

While it is acknowledged that the insights provided in this book may not serve as a panacea for all societal challenges, the aspiration is that my research journey catalyzes heightened awareness. I aspire to inspire others to recognize the plight of vulnerable individuals and societies, motivating them to take proactive measures to forge a better future for all.

Destination and Tourism Development

Tourism development orchestrates a symphony of factors, deftly utilizing destination resources and assets to sculpt indelible experiences tailored to the whims of tourists. This intricate dance not only caters to the transient desires of visitors but also ardently endeavors to uplift the quality of life for both the local residents and those journeying through. In this delicate balance, tourism emerges as a dynamic force, weaving a tapestry that intertwines the aspirations of travelers with the well-being of the communities they encounter. These factors can be categorized into four pivotal dimensions: economic, environmental, social, and cultural. These dimensions are intricately intertwined, exerting mutual influence on one another. Depending on the specific circumstances of a destination, these dimensions may either align harmoniously, come into conflict, or yield a blend of positive and negative outcomes. Understanding these nuances is key to determining whether tourism molds a destination's identity or merely reflects its existing characteristics.

Given the complex nature of these dimensions, it is imperative to establish precise definitions and comprehensive frameworks to guide research in this field. These foundational definitions serve as the bedrock for subsequent analysis and exploration, facilitating a deeper understanding of the intricate relationships between tourism development and overall well-being. Within the realm of tourism literature, destinations are often conceptualized as a construct composed of four interconnected components: space, mobility, social interaction, and economic value. These four facets collectively shape and define the essence of tourism experiences and their impact on both destinations and travelers. Let's explore each of these components to gain a more comprehensive understanding.

Space

In tourism, a "destination" is the focal point that encapsulates the location or space where tourism infrastructure, events, and services are concentrated. It serves as the very place where travelers find fulfillment for their needs and desires. The destination is a central issue within tourism studies, embodying in one single concept all the specific and problematic features of tourism, such as its systemic nature in which "space" plays a fundamental role.

When viewed through the lens of space, tourism underscores the central role that physical locations play in shaping the tourism experience. These spaces act as the canvases upon which travelers paint their memories, engage with local communities, and contribute to destinations' economic and cultural vitality. The exploration of "space and place" gained significant momentum among humanistic geographers during the 1970s. These two interrelated concepts elucidate how individuals perceive and engage with the natural world. Essentially, space represents an area devoid of inherent human meaning, awaiting the infusion of significance.

In contrast, places are imbued with meaning through human interactions and experiences.[6] Researchers from various disciplines recognized the profound impact of these human meanings on individuals' lives, sparking increased interest in the concept of place. The place is conceptualized through three primary constructs: location, locale, and sense of place.

---

[6] See, for example, Richards, G. (2023). Place, Culture, and Quality of Life. In Uysal, M. and Sirgy, M.J. (eds.) *Handbook of Tourism and Quality of life Research II.* Cham, Switzerland: Springer, p. 37-48. See also Licciardi, G. and Amirtahmasebi, R. (eds) (2012). *The economics of uniqueness.* Washington DC: The World Bank.

Among these constructs, the "sense of place" is relevant to social science research, as it delves into the intricate web of emotions, memories, and connections that individuals establish with specific locations.

The idea of a "sense of place" signifies the emotional connection that individuals establish with a specific geographic area. However, within the tourism domain, the term "place attachment" is more commonly utilized because it quantifies the intensity of one's connection rather than encompassing a broader emotional bond. Substantial research has proved that people can form strong affiliations with particular locations. These connections can evolve where individuals develop a sense of "ownership or possessiveness" towards the locale, sometimes leading to investments like timeshares or vacation homes. Place attachment is primarily structured around two fundamental dimensions: place identity and place dependence. Place identity pertains to individuals' emotional bond with a place, reflecting their profound sense of belonging and connection. On the other hand, place dependence gauges the degree to which a location is indispensable in delivering a unique experience, underscoring its distinct and irreplaceable value.

In tourism research, place attachment is a valuable instrument for understanding the dynamic between travelers and the destinations they select. When individuals establish deep connections with places, satisfaction is typically increased, and there is a greater likelihood of returning to the destination. Several factors, such as socio-demographics, involvement, and physical characteristics, have been identified as predictors of place attachment. Interestingly, there has been a notable omission in exploring how the travel experience contributes to this sense of attachment. Evaluating the quality or significance of the visitor experience may play a role in fostering place attachment. For example, we establish place attachment through several focus groups in Aruba.

It is imperative for both those responsible for planning destinations and intrepid explorers to comprehend the broad spectrum of spaces within the realm of tourism. The spaces individuals choose to visit are strongly shaped by their preferences, interests, and motivations. Some individuals seek solace and tranquility in natural settings, while others yearn for the exhilaration and cultural enrichment in bustling urban environments. Additionally, the accessibility and sustainability of these spaces are of significant importance for travelers and destination managers.

An alternative perspective on destinations reveals that they transcend mere geographical locations and function as intricate territorial systems. These systems are designed to provide at least one tourism product, comprising a bundle of goods and services with economic value. This product serves the intricate and multifaceted demands of tourism. However, it is crucial to acknowledge that this product is delicate, with characteristics such as perishability and seasonality. Unlike conventional goods, tourism experiences demand the physical presence of the consumer on-site, eliminating the possibility of separating production from consumption.

Unlike tangible goods that can be stored in inventory, tourism services are consumed as they are produced, rendering them highly perishable. Consider this scenario: a hotel manager finds themselves with unsold rooms at the end of the day. Compared to physical goods that can be carried over to the next day, these unsold rooms cannot be accumulated for future use. In simpler terms, if a hotel boasts 400 rooms but only manages to sell 200 on a given day, the remaining 200 cannot be carried forward to increase the hotel's capacity to 600 rooms the following day.

Furthermore, a destination's long-term viability heavily relies on its capacity to manage the influx of tourists within sustainable limits. Just as a delicate ecosystem thrives on balance, a destination's resilience hinges on its capacity to respond to fluctuating visitor numbers and resource demands dynamically. When a destination risks depleting its natural resources, it undermines its economic value and competitiveness in the market. This scenario often mirrors the tragedy of the commons, a concept frequently observed in tourism destinations worldwide.

In this complex ecosystem, tourists and residents vie for access to a limited pool of resources. Picture a pristine beach destination where locals rely on fishing for their livelihood while tourists flock to enjoy the picturesque shores. As tourist numbers surge, the demand for fish increases, leading to overfishing and the depletion of marine stocks. This not only jeopardizes the ecosystem's health but also compromises the sustainability of the fishing industry, upon which local communities depend.

Moreover, the strain on resources extends beyond environmental concerns to encompass social and cultural aspects. In destinations where historical sites and cultural landmarks draw visitors, overcrowding can erode the authenticity and charm that initially attracted tourists. Local communities may find themselves marginalized, grappling with inflated living costs and diminishing quality of life amidst the influx of tourists.

A destination is not merely a fixed point on the map but a dynamic crossroads where various elements converge. This includes the supply of hospitality services, diverse offerings, numerous activities, and many events. The physical space encompasses a broad spectrum of places individuals visit for leisure, exploration, or relaxation. These spaces exhibit remarkable diversity, ranging from the breathtaking beauty of pristine beaches and lush forests to the profound cultural significance of landmarks and historical sites. Even the bustling energy of urban centers finds its place within the overarching destination concept.

When we inspect tourism, it becomes evident that it is intricately interwoven with the spaces people explore and encounter during their journeys. Tourists are increasingly seen not just as consumers of destinations but as active participants capable of instigating change in cities and regions. This shift has led to an evolution in cultural and creative tourism strategies, moving from merely attracting high-quality tourists to engaging those who interact meaningfully with the destination and its people to enhance their well-being.[7]

---

[7] See, for example, Richards, G. (2023). Place, Culture, and Quality of Life. In Uysal, M. and Sirgy, M.J. (eds.) *Handbook of Tourism and Quality of life Research II.* Cham, Switzerland: Springer, p. 37-48.

Each destination is a unique tapestry of experiences waiting to be woven into the traveler's narrative, making the concept of tourism a fascinating exploration of both geography and human interaction. Destination Management Organizations (DMOs) are now focusing not only on distant tourists but also on permanent and temporary residents, recognizing that everyone can contribute to improving well-being. This perspective underscores that in tourism, well-being depends not only on a location's physical infrastructure and amenities but also on its users' presence, activities, and values.

In today's interconnected world, destinations are more than places on a map; they are vibrant ecosystems where cultures meet, exchanging ideas, and making memories. The interplay between tourists and the places they visit creates a dynamic environment where both the visitors and the destinations evolve. Tourists immerse themselves in local customs, cuisine, and traditions, contributing to a richer, more diversified experience for everyone involved. This symbiotic relationship between tourists and destinations fosters a sense of community and shared purpose, driving sustainable tourism practices that benefit all stakeholders.

Ultimately, a destination's essence lies in its ability to transform and be transformed by the people who experience it. Whether through the serene tranquility of natural landscapes or the lively buzz of city life, destinations offer endless possibilities for discovery and connection. The evolving strategies in tourism underscore the importance of inclusivity, cultural exchange, and mutual respect, ensuring that every journey positively impacts both the traveler and the place they visit.

Mobility

The pervasive nature of mobility in our modern world has transformed it into a coveted value, where the ability to move freely has become a defining feature of contemporary society. This unequal distribution of mobility has led to a stark division between those who possess it and those who do not, shaping our social reality into two distinct groups:

the mobile and the immobile. This division extends beyond theoretical constructs, manifesting in tangible ways in our daily lives, influencing where people live, their access to opportunities, and their overall quality of life. Consequently, this disparity in mobility has profound implications, impacting individuals, societies, and nations on a global scale. In essence, the unequal possession of mobility has become a defining characteristic of our era, with observable and far-reaching effects shaping our world.

Traditionally, tourism has been viewed as something separate from our daily lives, causing it to be somewhat marginalized within social sciences. Nevertheless, the perspective provided by the mobility paradigm presents an opportunity to reposition tourism as a central element of our social and cultural existence rather than a peripheral one. This paradigm underscores the importance of mobility within physical space as a fundamental means by which humans interact with the world, mold spatial perceptions, and shape the formation of places. It encompasses a range of social dynamics, including the movement of people, objects, and information.

By directing our focus toward mobility, a profound illumination emerges regarding the intricate interplay between the concept of freedom intertwined with travel and its pivotal role in shaping the contemporary tourism experience, particularly within specific contexts. This lens extends beyond mere mapping and comprehending large-scale global movements of people, goods, capital, and information. Advocates of the mobility paradigm emphasize that it encapsulates the nuanced and concurrent processes of daily commuting, navigating public spaces, and the movement of everyday objects. Delving into the environmental context reveals a critical discourse on sustainable and responsible travel, where the choices made in mobility reverberate beyond personal experiences, echoing in the ecological footprint of tourism destinations. Simultaneously, within the cultural context, the freedom of movement serves as a lens through which we can analyze the dynamic exchange of ideas, values, and traditions. Tourists engage with diverse societies and contribute significantly to destinations' cultural richness, creating a multifaceted tapestry woven by the threads of mobility and freedom.

Recognizing the pivotal role of tourist mobility is essential for effectively managing destinations, on-site movement planning, and strategically marketing attractions. Scholars and industry professionals have recently intensified their focus on understanding and leveraging tourist movement patterns. This involves applying sophisticated techniques such as market segmentation and behavior analysis to tailor tourism experiences according to visitors' diverse preferences and behaviors. The relationship between mobility and tourism unfolds across multiple dimensions, serving as the industry's very foundation. The ability to move is intrinsic to tourism, enabling individuals to visit varied destinations, immerse themselves in different cultures, and explore new places, whether for a brief weekend escape or an extensive international adventure.

Moreover, the economic impact of tourism is closely intertwined with mobility, mainly through air travel and road transportation. These modes of mobility play a pivotal role in facilitating the movement of tourists to diverse destinations, resulting in significant economic benefits for host communities. This includes job creation, revenue generation, and the flourishing of local businesses. Beyond economic aspects, mobility fosters cultural exchange by enabling interactions among people from diverse backgrounds. Tourists, driven by mobility, engage in cross-cultural encounters, immersing themselves in the languages, traditions, and lifestyles of the places they visit. However, this nexus between mobility and tourism also raises environmental concerns due to the substantial contribution of the transportation sector, necessitating a focus on sustainable options to mitigate the ecological footprint associated with travel.

Additionally, technological advancements in mobility have expanded the accessibility of destinations, and considerations related to mobility are paramount in planning and developing the infrastructure that underpins the tourism sector, encompassing airports, highways, public transportation systems, and accommodations. The COVID-19 pandemic laid bare the inherent vulnerabilities of the tourism industry, which relies heavily on the fluidity of human mobility. The abrupt imposition of international travel restrictions during the pandemic had cascading economic repercussions, causing widespread disruptions and losses within the tourism sector.

The COVID-19 pandemic delivered a jarring blow to the finely woven network of social interactions as travel destinations sealed their gates to tourists, grinding the entire industry to an unforeseen halt. In doing so, the pandemic laid bare the vulnerability of these intricate bonds. It shone a glaring spotlight on tourism's deep-seated influence over the complex web of global social dynamics.

The pandemic's disruptive force was keenly felt as bustling tourist hotspots turned eerily quiet, their streets and attractions devoid of the customary throngs of visitors. This sudden cessation of tourism activities served as a poignant reminder of the interdependence between the tourism sector and the socio-cultural fabric of host communities. It underscored how the livelihoods of countless individuals, from local artisans and service providers to hotel staff and tour guides, hinge on the influx of travelers.

Moreover, the pandemic raised profound questions about the environmental impact of tourism, as travel restrictions and lockdowns temporarily alleviated issues related to over-tourism, ecological degradation, and excessive carbon emissions associated with mass tourism. It prompted discussions on sustainable tourism practices and the need to balance economic growth and environmental conservation in the post-pandemic world.

Nevertheless, the crisis also catalyzed a wave of innovation to bolster the industry's resilience in the face of future challenges. This innovation manifested in the form of health and safety measures, with the adoption of contactless check-ins, the development of vaccine passports, and the integration of other technological solutions to mitigate risks associated with travel. These adaptive responses showcased the industry's capacity for resilience and illuminated the integral role of technology in shaping the future of tourism.

The profound interconnection between mobility and tourism extends beyond the economic dimension, encompassing cultural, environmental, and technological implications. Mobility, essentially the lifeblood of the tourism sector, has far-reaching effects on economies through job creation, revenue generation, and the growth of local businesses. However, it also poses challenges concerning its environmental impact, public health, and the need for sustainable practices and population health. As the world continues to evolve, the intricate dance between mobility and tourism is expected to redefine how we traverse the globe and experience diverse cultures. Striking a delicate balance between reaping the economic benefits of tourism and proactively addressing the environmental and societal challenges linked to increased mobility is paramount for the sustainable evolution of the industry.

Social Interaction

The emergence of the COVID-19 pandemic thrust the significance and essential nature of social interaction into the forefront of our consciousness. Tourism, a multifaceted phenomenon, can be best understood as a process and an outcome inherently intertwined with social interaction. People embark on journeys to new locales for many reasons, including cultural exploration, business pursuits, or to relish the offerings and services provided by a destination. However, tourism transcends the mere act of visiting places; it is fundamentally about engaging with people. Social interaction within tourism encompasses the bonds formed between travelers and local communities, fellow globetrotters, and those in the hospitality industry. These interactions play a pivotal role in enriching the tapestry of tourism experiences, fostering cultural exchange, empathy, and a profound comprehension of diverse societies.

Moreover, social interaction within the realm of tourism carries economic significance. As tourists increasingly seek distinctive and authentic experiences when choosing their destinations, their interactions with local populations become pivotal in defining and infusing meaning into these experiences. Consequently, the warmth and friendliness displayed by locals towards tourists and their willingness to integrate tourists into their daily lives can bestow potent and intangible attributes upon a destination and its people — attributes that are only realized through the firsthand experiences of tourists. These attributes, uniquely crafted by these interactions, ultimately shape the perceived value of a destination's distinctiveness.

In the dynamic realm of travel and tourism, the interplay between destination distinctiveness and the overall visitor experience forms a crucial nexus. Destination distinctiveness, rooted in a location's unique and defining attributes, serves as the foundational allure that captivates potential travelers. These distinctive features, from natural wonders, cultural richness, or historical significance, set a destination apart and render it appealing to those seeking novel and memorable experiences. Concurrently, the essence of a traveler's journey is encapsulated in the encompassing term "experience."[8] It encompasses the amalgamation of sensations, emotions, and memories that individuals accrue during their sojourn. The relationship between destination distinctiveness and experience is symbiotic, as a distinctive destination lays the groundwork for unique and memorable encounters and is shaped by the myriad of experiences it offers. Positive encounters contribute to the perceived distinctiveness of a destination, creating a feedback loop that influences the choices and preferences of future travelers. Marketing strategies often leverage a destination's distinctiveness to craft and promote specific experiences, aiming to attract a targeted audience seeking those unique qualities in their travel endeavors.

The willingness of residents to engage with tourists and the quality of these interactions are deeply rooted in how each resident perceives the

---

[8] See, for example, Pine, B. J., & Gilmore, J. H. (1999). *The experience economy: work is theatre & every business a stage*. Harvard Business Press. Rivera, M., Semrad, K., & Croes, R. (2015). The five E's in festival experience in the context of Gen Y: Evidence from a small island destination. *Revista Española de Investigación en Marketing ESIC (REIMKE)*, 19(2), 95-106.

impact of tourism development on their well-being. However, well-being is a complex concept that cannot be reduced to objective conditions, such as income and employment. Such traditional metrics may yield vastly different experiences for different individuals. Therefore, considering a subjective approach to measuring well-being may offer a more fruitful avenue for understanding the intricate relationship between tourism development, well-being, and small island destinations.

Moreover, social interaction is a vital antidote to the leveling influences of modern life, countering the tendency towards cultural homogenization and digitalization of human connections, provoking loneliness, and mental health issues. It operates as a potent catalyst for fostering a yearning to become acquainted with and understand others, offering the potential for transformative and enriching experiences. The roots of contemporary tourism can be traced back to progressive social policies that granted workers the privilege of annual paid holidays, thereby acknowledging the fundamental human right to leisure and respite from labor.[9] Beyond its extensively documented quantitative facets, tourism has evolved to encompass a profound cultural and moral dimension that merits nurturing and protection against any adverse distortions arising from economic pressures.

Additionally, the abrupt cessation of tourism activities exposed the intricate supply chains and global interconnectedness that underpin the industry. The pandemic's ripple effects were felt far and wide, from airlines and hotel chains to small-scale suppliers of locally sourced goods. It served as a stark reminder of how tourism is not confined to the destinations alone but is an integral part of the global economic tapestry. Furthermore, the pandemic's impact on tourism had cascading effects on cultural exchange and international understanding, prompting more social divisiveness. The absence of cross-cultural encounters and the suspension of tourism-related educational and exchange programs

---

[9] See, for example, Higgins-Desbiolles, F. (2006). More than an "industry": The forgotten power of tourism as a social force. *Tourism Management*, 27, 1192–1208.

highlighted the role of tourism as a conduit for fostering empathy, mutual understanding, and the exchange of ideas between people from diverse backgrounds.

Economic Value

Tourism stands as a formidable economic powerhouse, wielding substantial influence over the fortunes of numerous regions and nations across the globe. Its financial impact reverberates through a myriad of revenue streams, including but not limited to lodging, dining, transportation services, and the sale of goods and services that cater to the needs and desires of travelers. Yet, the worth of tourism transcends its immediate monetary gains, unfurling into a tapestry of far-reaching benefits. One of the foremost benefits is its capacity to spur job creation. The tourism sector is a vibrant source of employment, spanning a spectrum of roles from hotel staff and tour guides to artisans and local vendors.

The ripple effect of tourism-related employment extends to professionals within the sector and peripheral industries, enhancing overall economic resilience. For instance, consider the impact on the retail industry in a tourist destination. Local shops, markets, and boutiques experience increased foot traffic and sales as tourists indulge in shopping for souvenirs, local products, and cultural artifacts. This surge in demand bolsters individual retailers' livelihoods and contributes to the vitality of the broader local economy, creating a symbiotic relationship between tourism and peripheral industries.

Another noteworthy example of a peripheral industry thriving in the wake of tourism is the entertainment and cultural sector. As tourists seek authentic and immersive experiences, they often engage in cultural events, performances, and recreational activities unique to the destination. This heightened demand for cultural enrichment fosters the growth of theaters, museums, art galleries, music venues, and local attractions. Therefore, the entertainment and cultural sector experiences a surge in attendance and patronage, leading to increased employment opportunities for artists, performers, event organizers, and support staff. This adds to the diversity of experiences available to tourists and injects vitality into the local cultural scene. The economic impact extends beyond ticket sales, as visitors also contribute to the broader cultural ecosystem by purchasing related merchandise, artworks, and memorabilia. In this way, the symbiotic relationship between tourism and the entertainment and cultural sector exemplifies how peripheral industries can thrive by catering to travelers' diverse interests and preferences.

Simultaneously, tourism catalyzes infrastructure development. To accommodate the influx of visitors, destinations often embark on projects to enhance transportation networks, construct new accommodations, and improve public amenities. These investments elevate the tourism experience and contribute to the long-term growth and modernization of host regions. Foreign exchange inflow is another substantial advantage conferred by tourism. International visitors bring foreign currency, bolster a nation's reserves, and stabilize its economy. This foreign exchange inflow is particularly beneficial, as it can offset trade imbalances and contribute to a more robust economic outlook.

Tourism's impact transcends the surface-level contributions to local economies; it extends into the intricate web of global trade and economic interdependence. This is particularly evident in Spain's trajectory, where tourism has emerged as a pivotal force propelling economic transitions and sustainable development. The revenue generated by the influx of international visitors serves as a catalyst, creating a domino effect that fuels the hospitality and service sectors and stimulates a heightened demand for imported goods and services. This demand spans from luxury items to construction materials, fostering a dynamic that intricately weaves Spain into the fabric of the interconnected global economy. International tourism expands the domestic economy. International tourism boosts the domestic economy by injecting foreign currency and stimulating growth across various sectors while fostering cross-cultural exchange and innovation within domestic industries.

Spain's experience underscores how tourism can be a linchpin in financing broader economic shifts. The injection of substantial capital into the economy, driven by the country's status as a top tourist destination, provides the financial resources needed to diversify industries and embark on a journey toward more sustainable economic models. As Spain positions itself as an active participant in global trade, the nexus between tourism and economic development becomes increasingly apparent. In essence, Spain's story serves as a compelling narrative of how tourism can be a multifaceted driver beyond its immediate economic benefits, contributing to both local prosperity and broader international economic ties.[10]

For certain regions, particularly many developing countries, and numerous small island nations, tourism reigns supreme as the linchpin of their economic stability. This is the case for the islands of Aruba and Barbados, the dominant economic sector. These destinations heavily rely on the steady stream of visitors to sustain their livelihoods, making tourism an essential lifeline that keeps their economies afloat. Tourism's economic significance extends well beyond the surface, permeating various sectors, fostering employment, spurring development, and bolstering foreign exchange reserves. As a dynamic force that can drive economic growth, tourism remains an indispensable cornerstone for many developed and emerging nations in their quest for prosperity and progress.[11]

The global economic footprint of tourism is nothing short of staggering. Before the disruptive influence of the COVID-19 pandemic, the tourism industry stood as the most prominent service sector on the planet. It wielded immense influence, employing one in every ten individuals

---

[10] For the role of tourism in Spain's development achievements, see, for example, Jacint Balaguer & Manuel Cantavella-Jordá (2002) Tourism as a long-run economic growth factor: the Spanish case, *Applied Economics*, 34:7, 877-884, DOI: 10.1080/00036840110058923.

[11] See, for example, Croes, R. (2023). *Small Island and small destination tourism. Overcoming the smallness barrier for economic growth and tourism competitiveness.* Apple Academic Press: Waretown, NJ, USA.

worldwide, contributing to almost seven percent of all international trade, and representing a substantial 25 percent share of the world's service exports. This sector played a pivotal role as a crucial generator of foreign exchange. In 2019, its valuation soared to a staggering US$9 trillion, constituting 10.4 percent of the global Gross Domestic Product (GDP).

Tourism is a potent catalyst for economic diversification, presenting opportunities to cultivate new markets and bolster local economies. When managed thoughtfully, it fosters intricate local value chains, stimulating demand for existing and innovative products and services. This dynamic can bring about direct and positive effects on impoverished and remote communities, uplifting them through increased economic activity. Furthermore, the sector can play a pivotal role in championing broader societal and environmental causes, from preserving biodiversity to cultivating environmentally sustainable livelihoods. Positioned as a cornerstone of the burgeoning blue and green economy, tourism emerges as an economic force and a potential driver for positive social and environmental change. However, realizing this potential requires astute management to navigate associated risks and ensure that tourism's contributions remain net-positive for communities and ecosystems.

In stark contrast to the optimistic potential, the COVID-19 pandemic has dealt a severe blow to the tourism industry, disrupting livelihoods and economies on a global scale. The staggering loss of 62 million jobs, a shocking 20 percent of all tourism employment, and the plummeting of export revenue by US$1.3 trillion have sent shockwaves through the sector. The subsequent 50 percent reduction in the industry's contribution to the global GDP in 2020 alone underscores the profound impact. Small businesses, particularly women-led, are grappling with precarious circumstances, and communities heavily reliant on tourism face economic hardship. Additionally, governments must grapple with reduced tax revenues, constraining resources available for destination management, and preserving cultural and natural heritage sites.

Despite the formidable setback caused by the pandemic, the global tourism industry is poised for a remarkable resurgence, with ambitious expectations set for its economic prowess. Projections indicate that by the year 2033, the economic impact of tourism is primed to reach record-breaking heights, signifying a potential rebound and resurgence for an industry that has faced unprecedented challenges. This resurgence, however, calls for a delicate balance between revitalizing economic activity and implementing sustainable practices to ensure the long-term resilience of the tourism sector.

The World Travel and Tourism Council (WTTC), a prominent authority in the field, envisions a resounding resurgence in global travel spending over the coming decade. In this bright forecast, the tourism industry is anticipated to employ a substantial portion of the global workforce, accounting for nearly 12 percent of all employed individuals worldwide. This underscores the industry's enduring resilience and its role as a significant source of livelihoods across the globe.

According to the WTTC's comprehensive analysis, the tourism sector is poised to contribute substantially to the world's Gross Domestic Product (GDP). The forecast projects that by 2033, the industry will elevate its GDP contribution to a staggering US$15.5 trillion. This monumental leap marks a remarkable increase from its 2019 GDP contribution, which stood at US$10 trillion. This growth trajectory underscores the industry's potential to rebound and emerge stronger and more influential than ever before.

The anticipated resurgence of global tourism carries profound implications, not only for the industry itself but for the worldwide economy as a whole. It signals the capacity of this sector to drive economic recovery, stimulate job creation, and foster international collaboration and exchange. As the world sets its sights on a post-pandemic era, the tourism industry stands as a beacon of hope, promising a brighter and more prosperous future for countless individuals and communities worldwide.

Tourism Development

These four fundamental components of tourism are intricately interwoven, jointly shaping the intricate tapestry of the industry. Each element exerts its influence, with its interconnections manifesting in various ways that dictate tourism dynamics. Consider, for instance, the intimate relationship between space and mobility: the ease of accessing spaces, from remote natural wonders to bustling urban centers, is often contingent on the availability and efficiency of transportation modes. Social interaction, another crucial facet, can either elevate or diminish the overall tourism experience, casting ripples that affect the reputation of a destination. Concurrently, economic value plays a pivotal role in dictating the development and preservation of spaces and infrastructures, creating a feedback loop that reverberates through mobility and social interactions. When woven together, these four components coalesce to constitute the essence of tourism development.

Tourism development emerges as a broad and dynamic concept, weaving together diverse resources and assets to create a unique sense of place and identity that resonates with potential tourist markets. To achieve this, a complex orchestration involving various stakeholders and businesses is required, each playing a vital role in crafting a compelling tourism experience. At its core, tourism development unfolds through three fundamental dimensions: the identification and cultivation of appealing experiences or products (the What), the effective management of the creative process to bring these experiences to life (the How), and a deep understanding of the determinants influencing the tourist experience.

In delving into the "What" dimension, tourism development entails carefully selecting and crafting experiences or products with tremendous appeal within a specific environment. This involves a thoughtful consideration of the unique aspects that can captivate the imagination of potential visitors. Moving to the "How," effective creative process management becomes paramount in executing these offerings, ensuring they not only meet but exceed tourists' expectations. Finally, a profound understanding of the determinants involved in the tourist experience is crucial. The tourist experience is multifaceted, encompassing a blend of needs, motivations, and expectations. These factors drive tourists to seek destinations and activities that fulfill their desires and aspirations, shaping their overall perception of the travel experience. Understanding and catering to these elements is essential for destination management and ensuring visitor satisfaction. Experience goes beyond identifying what visitors seek; it involves recognizing the drivers shaping tourists' preferences and choices.

The dynamism within tourism development is accentuated by the perpetual evolution of production processes and the ever-shifting landscape of consumer preferences. This inherent dynamism necessitates a continuous process of societal learning, a journey shaped by the sentiments and perceptions of the residents intimately connected to the tourism development process. For instance, consider a picturesque coastal town that has traditionally thrived on its natural beauty and historical charm as a tourist destination. As societal preferences evolve, with an increasing emphasis on sustainable and immersive travel experiences, the residents play a pivotal role in steering the tourism development trajectory. Their insights, gathered from direct interactions with visitors and a deep understanding of the community's values, guide the transformation of tourism offerings. This collective learning process not only ensures that experiences align with contemporary preferences but also influences the development of initiatives that are not only more appealing but also more economically viable. In essence, societal learning becomes a cornerstone of successful tourism development, facilitating an ongoing adaptation and refinement that keeps the industry attuned to the ever-changing desires and expectations of residents and visitors.[12]

---

[12] For a discussion about the role of societal learning in tourism production, see Croes, R. (2023). *Small Island and small destination tourism. Overcoming the smallness barrier for economic growth and tourism competitiveness.* Apple Academic Press: Waretown, NJ, USA, chapter 2.

Tourism and Development

THE CONNECTION BETWEEN TOURISM AND DEVELOPMENT IS intricate, encompassing favorable and unfavorable aspects. Positively, tourism functions as a powerful catalyst for economic growth, the generation of employment, and the enhancement of infrastructure, thereby improving living standards in destination areas. Additionally, the cultural exchange facilitated by tourism contributes to understanding and tolerance among diverse communities, while the economic significance of tourism can motivate the preservation of natural and cultural heritage. However, the negative dimensions of this relationship are equally significant, as unregulated tourism may lead to environmental degradation, cultural erosion, and social inequalities. Dependence on tourism as a primary economic driver can also make destinations susceptible to external shocks. The essence of tourism lies in its ability to respect local contexts and yield positive returns. In essence, tourism not only adds value through productivity and growth but also enhances the quality of life and well-being. These combined attributes constitute the core of development.[13]

The allure of a destination often lies in its monumental landmarks, pristine beaches, and other attractions rather than its exports. The promotion of sustainable tourism, however, has a profound impact on the distribution of destination resources across various economic sectors. While tourism can generate income, foster development, and improve resident living

---

[13] Sharpley, R. and Telfer, D. (eds.), (2022). *Tourism and Development. Concepts and Issues.* Clevedon, UK: Channel View Publications.

standards, it diverts resources like labor from alternative economic opportunities for growth and sustenance. Furthermore, protecting natural resources, which are marketed to tourists, incurs costs that must be considered.

Despite tourism's prominent role in international trade, traditional international trade theories must address this phenomenon explicitly. The significance of tourism in international trade theories lies in its unique characteristic: tourists travel to destinations seeking amenities unavailable in their home countries. Tourism aligns with the flow of money, unlike merchandise trade. Tourists purchase amenities and services, contributing to a country's foreign exchange. This spending, therefore, functions as an export while the tourist's home country becomes an import. This dynamic has consequential economic effects, such as the tourism economic multiplier and its impact on the stability or instability of the balance of payments. The balance of payments, in turn, hinges on terms of trade, which reflects how export (tourist) prices change relative to import prices.

The central inquiry revolves around the factors causing disparities in costs and prices among different destinations. What lies beneath the variations in cost and price structures across destinations? Diverse theories within the realm of international trade aim to tackle these foundational questions, encompassing concepts like comparative advantage, the neo-classical factor endowment model, Linder and the demand-driven trade theory, and the endogenous comparative advantage framework.[14] Numerous pathways exist through which tourism positively impacts economic growth. Tourism serves as a substantial foreign exchange earner that supports capital investment. Additionally, it triggers investment in infrastructure and human capital and fosters healthy competition. The influence of tourism extends to other economic sectors through both

---

[14] See, Croes, R. and Marsiglio, S. (2022). Tourism in an open system: What do theories of international trade and competition teach us? In Croes, R. and Yang, Y. (eds.) *A Modern Guide to Tourism Economics*. Cheltenham, UK: Edward Elgar Publishing, Pages 37-58.

direct and indirect effects, contributing to overall economic stimulation. Furthermore, tourism is conducive to employment and income growth, generating economies of scale and scope. The combined effect of these channels underscores a mutually beneficial connection between tourism and economic development.

Furthermore, the theory of the linkage effect of the tourism industry suggests that tourism development can lead to the creation of linkages between the tourism industry and other sectors of the economy, such as agriculture, transportation, and construction. These linkages can generate additional economic benefits, such as increased employment and income. These theories suggest that tourism development can lead to economic growth by creating jobs and income, generating foreign exchange earnings, and stimulating development in other sectors of the economy. However, it is essential to note that the relationship between tourism development and economic growth is complex and can be influenced by various factors, including the destination's stage of development, the type of tourism being developed, and the policies and regulations in place.

In delving into the relationship between tourism and economic growth, my research aimed to answer a fundamental question: Can tourism be a driver of economic prosperity, and if so, how does this manifest? Recognizing income as a critical component of overall well-being, my studies sought to establish a nuanced connection between tourism and economic growth. The exploration extended beyond a macro-level analysis to ascertain whether the impact of tourism is felt directly at the household level. This inquiry formed a crucial part of the broader investigation into the tourism-led growth hypothesis.[15] By examining the intricate dynamics between tourism activities and economic indicators, the research aimed to uncover the nuanced pathways through which the tourism sector contributes to

---

[15] See, for example, Seetanah, B. et al. (2023). Tourism development and economic growth. In Croes, R. and Yang, Y. *A Modern Guide to Tourism Economics*. Cheltenham, UK.: Edward Edgar Publishing, Pages 152-169.

overall economic development and, more importantly, how it translates into tangible benefits for individual households.

The tourism-led growth hypothesis suggests that tourism development can catalyze economic growth by generating benefits, including employment, income, and foreign exchange earnings. At its core, the theory contends that the cumulative impact of tourism-related activities, such as job creation and increased income, can stimulate economic growth in a destination. This effect is particularly pronounced in developing countries, where tourism can play a pivotal role in fostering economic development. By attracting investment and catalyzing growth in sectors like agriculture, transportation, and construction, tourism contributes to a broader economic transformation. Empirical evidence supports the tourism-led growth hypothesis, with numerous studies showcasing a positive correlation between tourism development and economic growth in developing countries. Regions like the Caribbean and the Pacific report tourism as a major contributor to their GDP and a significant source of employment, reinforcing the idea that tourism can drive economic prosperity.

In 2003, Manuel Vanegas and I conducted a study where we validated the Tourism-Led Growth (TLG) model using Aruba as a case study.[16] Additionally, data from the World Travel and Tourism Council highlights Aruba and St. Lucia as nations highly specialized in tourism, showcasing remarkable real GDP per capita growth rates of 3.8% from 1986 to 2010, exceeding global averages by over double and outperforming OECD countries by nearly 2.5 times. Aruba particularly stands out within this cohort of countries for its exceptional performance.

However, the relationship between tourism development and economic growth is intricate and subject to various influencing factors. The stage of a destination's development, the type of tourism being pursued, and the

---

[16] See, for example, Croes, R. & Vanegas, M. (2003). Growth, development and tourism in a small economy: Evidence from Aruba. *International Journal of Tourism Research*, 5(5), 315-330.

regulatory framework in place can all impact the outcomes. Recognizing that not all tourist destinations can uniformly benefit from the tourism-led growth hypothesis is crucial. Some may experience adverse effects such as environmental degradation or social dislocation, underscoring the importance of implementing sustainable tourism management practices to maximize the positive impacts of tourism while mitigating potential drawbacks.

The tourism-led growth (TLG) hypothesis proposes a positive correlation between tourism development and economic growth, supported by studies I have conducted and referenced. Examining the distribution of this growth is of equal significance — whether it primarily benefits governmental entities or directly impacts households. For instance, in a collaborative study on tourism specialization in Malta, findings indicated a significant portion of income directly benefiting households, thus influencing human development indicators such as health and education.[17] While tourism development can yield positive and negative effects across economic, environmental, social, and cultural realms, it's imperative to discern whether tourism acts as a formative or reflective construct to select the most appropriate assessment methodologies.

The Criticality of Tourism Specialization

The economic growth perspective on tourism posits that focusing on tourism specialization directly contributes to positive economic growth, subsequently enhancing the overall quality of life.[18] However, this viewpoint is fraught with challenges. Firstly, the assumed consistently positive relationship between tourism specialization and economic growth may not hold over time, introducing an element of unpredictability and

---

[17] See, for example, Croes, R., Van Niekerk, M., & Ridderstaat, J. (2018). Tourism specialization and quality of life: Evidence from Malta. *Tourism Management,* 68, 212-223.
[18] See, for example, Chapter 2 of Croes, R. (2023). *Small Island and Small Destination Tourism. Overcoming the Smallness Barrier for Economic Growth and Tourism Competitiveness.* Palm Bay, Florida: Apple Academic Press.

volatility into the equation. Secondly, this perspective adopts a narrow and instrumental understanding of the quality of life, equating it solely with economic growth. This reductionist viewpoint oversimplifies a multifaceted concept, neglecting other crucial aspects contributing to a comprehensive well-being assessment. Furthermore, the prevalent literature in tourism often prioritizes revenues as the primary metric, emphasizing expenditures as the critical determinant of success.

Simply focusing on tourism receipts offers an incomplete assessment of a destination's potential, neglecting crucial qualitative factors that shape the experiences of both visitors and residents. It is vital to understand that evaluating a destination's success shouldn't solely revolve around revenue generation. Instead, destination managers should adopt a holistic approach, considering the broader impact on the local community's well-being. Relying strictly on revenue without acknowledging its effects on residents may lead to adverse outcomes, as evidenced by findings from studies in Malaysia and Costa Rica. In Malaysia, challenges in institutional frameworks hindered the equitable distribution of benefits, while in Costa Rica, issues of inequality played a significant role, underscoring the importance of a balanced and sustainable approach to tourism development.

The relationship between tourism specialization and economic growth is intricate and sometimes straightforward, with market failures and complicating factors potentially impeding a direct positive connection. An illustrative example of market failure in the tourism context arises when there is insufficient information about the environmental impact of certain tourist activities. Without comprehensive information, tourists and businesses in a destination may not make decisions aligned with sustainable practices, leading to a failure of the market to account for negative externalities such as environmental degradation, overexploitation of natural resources, habitat destruction, and pollution. Without mechanisms internalizing the ecological costs, market forces may not effectively promote sustainable practices, indicating a scenario of market failure. Addressing this requires interventions like regulations, certifications, and public awareness campaigns to align behavior with sustainable principles.

Studies exploring the relationship between tourism specialization and economic growth yield inconsistent results. While some report a positive association, others find no discernible relationship or even a non-linear connection that starts positively but turns negative due to diminishing returns. Even if empirical evidence supports a direct positive relationship between tourism specialization and economic growth over time, the assumption that economic growth automatically results in improved well-being oversimplifies reality. The understanding of quality of life has shifted from a one-dimensional focus on income to a multi-dimensional interpretation, recognizing factors such as life expectancy, education, social support, and freedom. Scholars like Amartya Sen have emphasized a capability-focused approach considering various factors shaping individuals' capabilities and freedoms.[19]

The traditional one-dimensional understanding of well-being has evolved towards a multi-dimensional interpretation, acknowledging that income is only one aspect of well-being. Other crucial factors include life expectancy, education, social support, and freedom. Sen's capability-based approach shifts the focus from income as the sole determinant of well-being. Tourism specialization, measured by international tourism receipts about the gross domestic product, correlates positively with economic growth in some countries. However, the impact on residents' well-being remains to be determined, as increased income from tourism specialization may benefit some at the expense of others, making it challenging to determine if the effects on residents' well-being will be positive.

Two potential causal relationships between tourism specialization and well-being emerge as significant considerations. As outlined in the study, human activity's fundamental objective is to augment people's choices, thereby fostering creativity and productivity — crucial factors

---

[19] Sen, A. (1999). *Development as freedom*. Oxford: Oxford University Press.

contributing to economic growth and exports. A notable connection is established between tourism specialization and well-being. On the one hand, tourism specialization is identified as a potential resource conducive to maintaining high well-being. Conversely, an improvement in well-being can reciprocally contribute to increased tourism specialization.

The notion that well-being serves as the paramount goal of tourism development reverberates throughout the tourism literature. This perspective aligns seamlessly with mainstream development theory, emphasizing that residents are vested in any economic activity, including tourism, capable of enhancing their well-being. In my work, well-being is conceptualized as a multidimensional construct, encompassing objective factors like health, education, and income and an individual's subjective assessment of life experiences. Well-being is defined here as a composite of material and non-material aspects, evaluated through conventional utility measurements and the capability approach. The capability approach, as emphasized in the study, positions the individual as the ultimate goal of development, portraying development as the process of expanding people's choices and opportunities in life.

The relationship between tourism specialization, economic growth, and well-being is intricate and influenced by various factors that differ across countries. The development of tourism specialization is unique, with the country's economic structure, institutional capabilities, ability to address market failures, quality of human capital, and the dynamic nature of specialization all playing pivotal roles. These factors collectively determine the quality of growth and its impact on residents' well-being. Constraints related to these factors may limit tourism's ability to drive growth and improve the well-being of residents. Furthermore, the effect of tourism can vary significantly based on the stage of the community in the tourism development life cycle, which includes phases such as introduction, growth, stagnation, rejuvenation, or decline. Research indicates that the relationship between tourism numbers (arrivals and expenditures) and economic contributions to residents' well-being needs to be clarified. While tourism specialization may have positive effects, it can also negatively affect residents' well-being.[20]

The literature on tourism presents an inconclusive picture regarding the effects of tourism specialization on residents' well-being. Well-being is a foundational consideration for development options, providing a framework for assessing the potential benefits and drawbacks of tourism specialization for residents. However, most studies on well-being have primarily focused on residents in developed or large countries, leaving a gap in our understanding, particularly for small island destinations. Small islands face unique challenges due to limited resources and economic opportunities, making them unable to afford costly development mistakes. Understanding the intricacies of residents' well-being and its connection to tourism specialization is crucial for the socio-economic future of small islands. This relationship is not just a theoretical question; it is empirically relevant, especially for small islands that must judiciously use their scarce resources to ensure their residents' high quality of life. Acknowledging the limits of how much tourism specialization can sustain growth and enhance the quality of life is paramount for informed decision-making in the context of these unique and resource-constrained destinations.

Critical Questions

Tourism is traveling to and staying in places outside one's usual environment for leisure, business, or other purposes. It is a multi-billion-dollar industry that plays a significant role in the economy of many countries. It encompasses various activities such as sightseeing, adventure travel, cultural exchange, and relaxation. It can also be classified into different types: domestic tourism (travel within one's own country) and international tourism (travel to other countries).

Tourism can have both positive and negative effects on a destination. On

---

[20] There is a plethora of excellent works in Uysal. M. and Sirgy, M.J. (2023). *Handbook of Tourism and Quality of life Research II*. Cham, Switzerland: Springer.

the positive side, it can generate economic benefits by creating jobs and generating income through visitor spending. It can also promote cultural exchange and understanding and preserve historical and natural sites. However, tourism can also lead to adverse effects such as overcrowding, environmental degradation, and displacement of local communities.

The concept of sustainable tourism has emerged to address these adverse effects by promoting responsible and equitable tourism practices that balance economic, social, and environmental considerations. This approach aims to create long-term benefits for tourists and local communities while minimizing negative impacts. Tourism is a complex and dynamic field involving many different stakeholders and requires careful planning and management to achieve sustainable and equitable outcomes.

These investigations form part of a larger body of research known as the Tourism-Development-Growth nexus. This field explores the interdependencies and interactions among tourism development, economic growth, and overall development outcomes. By examining the empirical evidence and conducting rigorous analyses, I aimed to contribute to understanding how tourism can serve as a catalyst for economic growth and its subsequent implications for the well-being of individuals and communities.

Ultimately, by establishing a solid foundation for the positive relationship between tourism development and economic growth, I aimed to provide insights that inform policy and decision-making processes. Understanding the intricate mechanisms and channels through which tourism contributes to economic prosperity allows for more targeted and effective interventions to maximize the benefits of tourism development for various stakeholders, ultimately enhancing overall well-being.

The Tourism-led growth (TLG) hypothesis suggests a positive correlation between tourism development and economic growth, a widely accepted and validated proposition in existing literature. My research delved into multiple studies aimed at comprehensively exploring this relationship, identifying three pivotal factors contributing to economic growth within the framework of tourism development. First and foremost, the feedback loop mechanism emerged as a crucial element. This dynamic suggests that as tourism develops, it stimulates economic activities, generating income and employment opportunities and fostering further tourism growth. This cyclical process forms a self-reinforcing mechanism where tourism and economic growth mutually propel each other.

Secondly, the research looked into tourism development's short- and long-term effects on economic growth. Beyond immediate economic impacts, such as increased tourist expenditures and business revenues, enduring effects contribute to sustained growth. Long-term benefits may include infrastructure development, skill enhancement among the local workforce, and an enhanced business environment, all instrumental in fostering economic growth over time. Aruba, a Caribbean island nation, provides a compelling example of tourism development's short- and long-term effects on economic growth. In the short term, Aruba experiences a surge in tourist expenditures, with visitors contributing significantly to the local economy through spending on accommodations, dining, entertainment, and recreational activities. The immediate economic boost created a flourishing hospitality sector and generated employment and business opportunities for the local population.

In the long term, the sustained growth in tourism has prompted substantial investments in infrastructure development on the island. Aruba has focused on enhancing its tourism-related facilities, including modernizing airports, expanding cruise ship terminals, and upgrading public amenities. These long-term investments cater to the increasing number of tourists and position Aruba as a competitive and attractive destination, fostering economic growth over an extended period. Moreover, the continuous influx of tourists has catalyzed skill development among the local workforce. The demand for diverse services has led to the cultivation of expertise in hospitality, language proficiency, and cultural understanding. This ongoing skill enhancement ensures a high service standard for visitors and contributes to the local workforce's overall development, creating a sustainable foundation for economic growth.

Additionally, the thriving tourism industry in Aruba has spurred the growth of ancillary businesses and entrepreneurial ventures. Local entrepreneurs have capitalized on the demand for tourism by establishing businesses such as souvenir shops, water sports facilities, and authentic culinary experiences. This diversified business landscape adds vibrancy to the local economy and ensures resilience by reducing dependence on a single sector.

Additionally, the study explored the concept of dynamic elasticities within the relationship between tourism and economic growth. It recognized that the impact of tourism development on economic growth is not static; instead, it evolves and adapts to changing circumstances. This relationship's elasticity reflects economic growth's responsiveness to changes in tourism development, accounting for various factors such as policy interventions, technological advancements, and shifts in consumer behavior. Understanding the dynamic elasticities inherent in the tourism-economic growth nexus is crucial for policymakers and industry stakeholders in formulating strategies that maximize the positive outcomes of tourism development on economic growth.

Tourist demand is influenced by factors within and beyond the destination's control, such as income elasticity in the tourists' home countries and the quality of the tourism product. Income elasticity of demand in the source country refers to how changes in income levels of tourists' home countries affect their demand for tourism-related goods and services. For example, if the income in a particular country rises, its residents may have more disposable income available for travel, leading to an increase in demand for international tourism. Conversely, during economic downturns, people may cut back on discretionary spending, including travel, resulting in a decrease in demand for tourism services. For instance, when a country's economy experiences significant growth, such as in China in recent years, its citizens often have more resources to spend on international travel, contributing to a surge in global tourism demand. Conversely, during periods of economic recession, such as the global financial crisis 2008 2009, international tourism tends to contract as consumers tighten their belts and prioritize essential expenditures over leisure travel.

Tourism demand is intricately tied to the quality of a destination's product. Take, for example, the remarkable rise of Iceland as a tourism hotspot in recent years, driven by its unique natural attractions like geysers and glaciers. By capitalizing on its pristine landscapes and offering adventurous activities such as glacier hiking and whale watching, Iceland has successfully attracted travelers seeking authentic and unforgettable experiences. Conversely, destinations lacking compelling tourism offerings may need help to draw visitors, highlighting the importance of continually investing in enhancing and diversifying the tourism product to remain competitive in the global market.

As time progresses, the elasticity of demand for tourist products may decline, signaling diminishing returns once a certain income threshold is reached in the source country. This highlights the significance of delving into segmentation opportunities within affluent nations. Conversely, the tourism industry exhibits a unique supply dynamic distinct from manufacturing, where supply must consistently align with demand. High demand or restricted availability frequently influences tourism supply, resulting in gradual growth. For instance, small island destinations grapple with supply constraints such as limited land, accommodation capacity, and environmental resources, which significantly shape their approach to tourism development strategies.

Segmentation opportunities within affluent countries offer avenues to enhance income elasticity in tourism. For example, luxury tourism targeting high-income individuals can increase spending per tourist, thereby boosting overall tourism revenue. By catering to niche markets such as eco-tourism or adventure travel, destinations can attract affluent travelers willing to pay premium prices for unique experiences, thereby augmenting income elasticity. Another example is spiritual tourism.

Spiritual tourism offers a compelling opportunity for destinations to enhance income elasticity within the tourism sector. This niche market caters to travelers seeking spiritual or religious experiences, such as pilgrimages or visits to sacred sites. For example, destinations like Varanasi in India and Lourdes in France attract millions of pilgrims annually, contributing significantly to the local economy through spending on accommodations, food, and donations. Tapping into spiritual tourism allows destinations to diversify their visitor base and stimulate economic growth while providing travelers with meaningful and transformative experiences.

These findings contribute to a nuanced understanding of the diverse relationship between tourism development and economic growth, offering insights that can inform more targeted and effective policy measures in tourism-led economic development. Moving on to the second set of questions, it becomes crucial to understand where precisely this economic growth generated by tourism goes. Does it primarily flow into the government's coffers, giving them the authority to decide how to utilize the funds and allocate them appropriately? Or does a significant portion of this growth directly benefit households? If the latter is true, it becomes essential to examine the implications regarding vital aspects of the Human Development Index (HDI), such as health, education, income distribution, access to basic services, employment opportunities, social inclusion, and gender equality.

The Nature of Tourism Development

Exploring the intricate relationship between tourism and poverty has been a compelling journey that resonates with my passion for addressing vulnerability. Our research, conducted across diverse contexts in Mexico, Ecuador, Nicaragua, Costa Rica, and Colombia, sought to unveil the complexities of this connection and shed light on tourism's potential to mitigate poverty.

Our initial findings showed a clear and positive correlation between tourism development and poverty reduction. Employing the standard set by the United Nations Development Program, where individuals earning less than $1 per day are deemed to be living in absolute poverty, we discerned that tourism played a pivotal role in alleviating such dire economic conditions. This insight offered a broad understanding of the overall positive impact of tourism on poverty. Yet, recognizing the multifaceted nature of this relationship, we delved deeper to unravel the nuanced mechanisms through which tourism effectively contributed to poverty reduction.

Furthermore, our research revealed that the issue of inequality extended beyond income disparities. Spatially, there were also disparities between urban and rural areas, which further compounded the problem. These observations emphasized the multidimensional nature of the challenges posed by inequality in the context of tourism development. Considering the implications of these findings, it became crucial to examine how individuals affected by these circumstances perceived the situation. Understanding the perspectives and sentiments of the people involved played a vital role in capturing the complete picture of the impact of tourism on poverty and inequality.

Our research focused on examining the opportunities available to individuals and how they seized those opportunities, ultimately exploring their impact on their living conditions. It became evident that inequality played a significant role in determining the opportunities one could access based on one's place of birth and the urban or rural environment one inhabited. This spatial context heavily influenced the available opportunities individuals could pursue. However, our investigation went beyond the objective circumstances and examined the subjective experiences and feelings of the individuals affected.

We sought to understand how they perceived their life conditions and the overall experiences they encountered. The results we obtained were intriguing and shed light on a complex dynamic. Despite facing challenging life conditions, the poor in these countries reported feeling happy. However, an important distinction emerged when we considered their satisfaction with life. In this context, happiness seemed to be a more fleeting and emotional response. At the same time, satisfaction with life appeared to be a more cognitive evaluation of one's overall well-being over a longer-term perspective. This dichotomy between happiness and satisfaction with life posed an interesting paradox.

Attempting to explain this phenomenon required careful consideration. It highlighted the nuanced interplay between emotional well-being and cognitive evaluation of one's life circumstances. The coexistence of happiness and dissatisfaction with life among the poor demonstrated that subjective well-being is influenced by various factors beyond material conditions alone. Our findings revealed a complex and broad understanding of how individuals experienced and evaluated their life conditions, navigating a delicate balance between happiness and long-term satisfaction with life.

The nature of employment in the tourism industry, often characterized by seasonal fluctuations, profoundly impacts the emotional and experiential landscape of individuals in these roles. At the outset, the availability of seasonal jobs brings joy and satisfaction to those who secure such positions, providing them with a means of income and job security. However, this happiness is fleeting, giving way to the inevitable reality of job loss as the seasons change, creating a cyclical pattern that individuals navigate repeatedly.

The cyclical nature of seasonal tourism jobs not only influences individuals' immediate emotions but also profoundly impacts their long-term life aspirations. The repetitive employment and job loss pattern creates a narrative of limited professional growth and financial stability. Individuals in these positions, adapting to the temporality of their work, often find themselves discouraged from pursuing ambitious long-term goals. The constant uncertainty surrounding employment hampers their ability to envision a stable and upward career trajectory. For instance, a hotel worker employed during peak tourist seasons may experience job security and contentment during those periods but face the looming uncertainty of unemployment during off-peak times. This cycle can instill a sense of resignation, leading individuals to prioritize short-term stability over long-term aspirations, thereby shaping their career trajectories and limiting their ability to break free from the cycle of seasonal employment.

Recognizing the impact of seasonal tourism jobs' cyclical nature on individuals' long-term aspirations highlights crucial policy implications. Depending solely on surveys indicating momentary happiness among those employed in seasonal positions may lead to a misguided sense of contentment in policymaking. Political leaders interpreting these survey results at face value might erroneously assume that immediate satisfaction implies no further action is necessary.

Neglecting the complexities linked to the temporary nature of tourism sector employment results in an oversimplified approach that fails to grasp individuals' broader challenges concerning job stability and career development. Policymakers must move beyond superficial and generic indicators and acknowledge the dire realities of seasonal employment dynamics. Effective policies demand a thorough understanding of the nuanced nature of such employment, ensuring initiatives are tailored to address the intricate situations encountered by workers in the tourism industry. An objective assessment would reveal that a substantial percentage of the population, for instance, 30%, lives on or below $1 a day. It is unreasonable to conclude that individuals with such limited means lead fulfilling lives and function well. Therefore, concurrently analyzing objective indicators and subjective experiences is essential for a comprehensive understanding. Failing to do so may result in erroneous conclusions and subsequent adverse consequences.

A balanced approach considering both perspectives is crucial for informing effective policymaking and addressing the underlying challenges faced by individuals in the tourism industry. The realization that individuals' feelings of happiness and satisfaction, or lack thereof, can significantly impact their overall well-being led us to an important question: How does this dynamic affect tourism development? If individuals are not completely satisfied with their lives, it implies potential health, education, and productivity issues. These factors can hinder their ability to contribute effectively to the tourism sector, ultimately impacting its growth and development. It became evident that the relationship between well-being and tourism is bidirectional: Not only does tourism influence well-being, but well-being also influences the success and progress of the tourism industry.

Understanding well-being as both an outcome and a driving force in tourism development is crucial. A study conducted by Jorge Ridderstaat and myself reveals four key mechanisms through which well-being influences tourism development.[21] Firstly, residents' positive attitudes and support towards tourists foster a welcoming environment, facilitating further tourism growth. Secondly, initiatives to enhance destination residents' well-being, such as cultural projects, indirectly benefit tourism by offering enriching experiences. Thirdly, education correlates with improved well-being, enabling individuals to contribute more effectively to the tourism product. Lastly, residents' attempts to exploit tourists for personal gain can harm tourism development despite potential benefits to individual well-being. These findings highlight the dynamic role of well-being in shaping the trajectory of tourism development. Recognizing the impact of well-being on talent, productivity, and overall performance is vital for attracting and retaining skilled individuals who can contribute to the growth of the tourism sector. Therefore, focusing on holistic development and well-being is imperative to create an environment conducive to flourishing tourism.

Dynamic Tourism Development

With this insight, we examined how these dynamics unfolded in different locations. Starting with the Caribbean islands, we sought to compare and analyze their performance based on objective criteria such as tourism

---

[21] Ridderstaat, J., Croes, R., & Nijkamp, P. (2016). A two-way causal chain between tourism development and quality of life in a small island destination: An empirical analysis. *Journal of Sustainable Tourism*, 24(10), 1461-1479.

arrivals, the Human Development Index, GDP, and population. The comparative analysis examined these indicators and aimed to identify factors contributing to these islands' varying performance levels. By scrutinizing the data, we aimed to uncover the underlying factors and strategies that explain why some Caribbean islands outperformed others. This examination went beyond mere statistical comparisons and inspected each location's contextual nuances and unique circumstances. The goal was to identify successful practices and approaches that can be replicated or adapted to enhance tourism development and improve overall well-being in other destinations.

Our exploration of the relationship between GDP and the Human Development Index (HDI) unveiled the intricate interplay of economic indicators influenced by tourism activities, subsequently impacting community development. The HDI, rooted in the capability approach introduced by a Nobel Prize winner in the late 1970s or 1980s, is a comprehensive measure of human development. When scrutinizing countries with the highest income per capita and the highest HDI, a diminishing trend emerges, showcasing that beyond a certain GDP threshold, further increases do not necessarily translate into a corresponding improvement in HDI (See Figure 1). This observation underscores that income alone fails to encapsulate the complete narrative, emphasizing the diverse factors influencing the human development index.

Revisiting the importance of both objective indicators and subjective experiences, we redirected our focus to individuals' sentiments about their lives. Developing hypotheses centered on the factors within tourism development that may impact resident satisfaction and overall well-being became imperative. These hypotheses can be broadly categorized into two types. The first hypothesis posits that tourism development directly influences residents' satisfaction with personal life. Simultaneously, the second hypothesis proposes that tourism development directly and indirectly affects residents' satisfaction through various life situations, reflecting the interconnectedness of tourism activities with broader aspects of residents' well-being.

Tourism development grapples with a dual challenge, marked by the issues of fragmentation and coordination within the industry. Fragmentation refers to more integration and cooperation among diverse segments like tour operators, travel agents, hotels, airlines, and destination management organizations. This absence of synergy can result in coordination problems, such as a need for more information sharing, conflicting policies, and a lack of standardization. Consequently, inefficiencies arise, and the consistency of the services offered to tourists becomes compromised, adversely affecting the tourism experience.

Figure 1 The concave relationship between Income and HDI

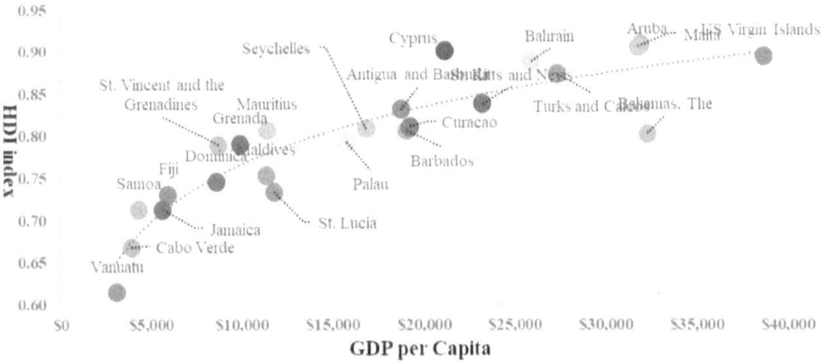

Source: Author's own creation

The lack of information sharing among different stakeholders in the tourism industry is a prominent issue associated with fragmentation. Tourists may need help finding accurate and comprehensive information about destinations or travel options, while suppliers face challenges in effectively marketing their products. Conflicting policies among stakeholders can lead to clarity and satisfaction among tourists and impede the creation and implementation of effective marketing strategies by suppliers and destinations.

Standardization, or the lack thereof, is another significant problem stemming from fragmentation in the tourism industry. Varying policies and procedures among different suppliers and destinations can result in clarity and consistency in the quality of service provided to tourists. This diversity makes it challenging for tourists to compare options and make informed decisions about their travel plans.

The challenges of fragmentation and coordination in the tourism industry can contribute to inefficiencies and inconsistencies that harm the overall tourism experience. Stakeholders within the industry must collaborate to address these issues, fostering information sharing, coordinating policies, and promoting standardization to enhance the quality of service provided to tourists and elevate the tourism experience. Researchers like Candela and Figini have explored the coordination problem in tourism, shedding light on its causes and proposing potential solutions.[22] They emphasize that a lack of communication and cooperation among different stakeholders is at the core of the coordination problem, resulting in conflicting policies and a need for more consistency in service quality.

Candela and Figini also highlight the importance of standardization in addressing the coordination problem in tourism. They argue that standardization can help to improve the overall quality of service provided to tourists by ensuring that different suppliers and destinations have consistent policies and procedures. Additionally, Candela and Figini have proposed using technology to solve the coordination problem in tourism. They suggest that technology can be used to facilitate communication and cooperation among different stakeholders in the tourism industry, as well as to promote standardization. They also propose using digital platforms to share information and coordinate policies among various stakeholders.

The coordination problem within the tourism industry can lead to an "anti-commons" situation characterized by too many stakeholders with competing interests, each possessing the ability to obstruct or impede progress. In tourism, this scenario unfolds when various industry segments, such as tour operators, travel agents, hotels, airlines, and

---

[22] See, for example, Candela, G. and Figini, P. (2012). *The economics of tourism destinations*. Dordrecht: Springer.

destination management organizations, exhibit conflicting interests and are unwilling or unable to collaborate.

This anti-commons situation often results in a gridlock, where progress is hampered or completely halted. For instance, a lack of cooperation among different stakeholders can hinder the development of effective marketing strategies and impede creating a seamless and consistent tourist experience.

Consider a destination struggling with conflicting interests between tour operators and hotels. Tour operators may prioritize cost-effective packages to attract budget-conscious tourists, while hotels may aim for high-end clientele, emphasizing luxury and exclusivity. This misalignment can lead to a disjointed marketing approach and an inconsistent tourist experience, as the destination needs to present a cohesive and appealing image. The gridlock created by the anti-commons situation impedes the industry's ability to enhance the overall tourism experience collectively. Addressing such challenges requires fostering collaboration and shared objectives among stakeholders to break the gridlock and facilitate more cohesive and effective strategies for tourism development.

In upcoming chapters, I will examine the importance of tackling fragmentation and coordination issues to improve residents' well-being. However, before delving into practical strategies, I will first explore the foundational concepts of well-being in the following chapter.

The Broadening Concept of the Human Welfare Paradigm

THE CONCEPT OF MULTIDIMENSIONAL WELL-BEING ENCOMPASSES diverse interpretations, spanning from feelings of contentment, pleasure, and material comforts to a profound sense of meaning and purpose. Definitions of well-being inherently involve an evaluative process, wherein positive aspects are contrasted with negative ones, reflecting the distinction between well-being and illbeing, the former being desirable and the latter undesirable.

This evaluative process is not limited to a singular dimension but extends across various facets of an individual's life. It involves a comprehensive assessment wherein individuals globally evaluate their lives across diverse aspects. This assessment revolves around understanding the "what" and the "how" of well-being. The "what" pertains to the object of evaluation, which includes an individual's emotional and cognitive states and their revealed and expressed preferences. In essence, the assessment of multidimensional well-being delves into the nuanced exploration of subjective experiences and cognitive appraisals, employing diverse criteria and measurements to gauge the overall quality of an individual's life.

While exploring this topic, I initially approached well-being through a material lens. As an applied economist, my focus centered on tangible foundations such as income and basic needs to address the physical aspect of well-being. However, it is imperative to acknowledge that well-being extends beyond material wealth and encompasses opportunities and the pursuit of those opportunities. Equally significant is the subjective perspective that influences how individuals feel about these opportunities. This plays a crucial role in defining overall well-being.

The term "well-being" encompasses a comprehensive state of being healthy, comfortable, and content, spanning physical, mental, and emotional health. Moreover, it includes factors such as social connections and overall life satisfaction, presenting a broader perspective beyond illness's mere absence. Despite its wide scope, critics argue that well-being is challenging to measure universally. Different cultures and individuals may have varied notions of what constitutes well-being, which emphasizes the subjective nature of the concept and the necessity to consider personal values and beliefs when assessing an individual's well-being. Furthermore, critiques highlight that the current definition often concentrates on the individual, neglecting larger societal and environmental factors that influence overall well-being. Some argue that the focus is skewed towards the absence of illness, overlooking positive attributes like connection, purpose, and personal growth. From an economic viewpoint, well-being is often measured through a person's standard of living, incorporating income, wealth, and resource access.

While widely used, traditional metrics like GDP and GNP are criticized for overlooking factors such as income inequality, environmental degradation, and social capital. Alternatives like the Human Development Index (HDI) and the Genuine Progress Indicator (GPI) have been proposed to provide a more comprehensive evaluation of economic well-being by considering health, education, environmental, and social factors.

The Shift to a Multidimensional Concept

Despite a noticeable increase in studies addressing well-being, the lack of a precise definition poses a challenge to effective measurement, which hinders its application to human welfare. Well-being emerges as a pivotal and relevant tool in policymaking, offering a comprehensive framework that extends beyond traditional economic metrics. By integrating well-being considerations into policy decisions, governments can pursue holistic objectives encompassing health, education, social connections, and personal fulfillment. This approach ensures a more nuanced understanding of the diverse factors contributing to a high quality of life. Well-being metrics provide valuable insights for informed resource allocation, enabling policymakers to target investments in areas that significantly improve people's lives.

Moreover, a well-being-oriented approach promotes long-term sustainability by addressing environmental, social, and economic dimensions. A prime example of a well-being-oriented approach promoting long-term sustainability is the ecotourism initiatives in Costa Rica. By prioritizing the conservation of its rich biodiversity, empowering local communities, and fostering sustainable economic growth through tourism, Costa Rica has established itself as a global leader in ecotourism. This holistic approach not only preserves the natural environment but also enhances social well-being by providing economic opportunities for residents while offering authentic and immersive experiences for visitors. As a result, Costa Rica has achieved significant success in balancing environmental preservation with economic development, ensuring the long-term sustainability of its tourism industry.

Policies geared towards well-being emphasize preventive measures in healthcare and social interventions, reducing the need for reactive and costly measures. The inclusive nature of well-being-focused policies fosters social cohesion, reduces inequality, and promotes adaptability to changing circumstances. Overall, prioritizing well-being in policymaking not only creates resilient and sustainable societies but also garners public engagement and trust, which helps ensure the successful implementation of measures that genuinely enhance the overall welfare of citizens.

Considering the growing interest in evaluating well-being within mainstream tourism literature, there is a pressing need to establish a clear and consistent definition. The term "well-being" is used interchangeably to describe various facets of life, such as quality of life, happiness, and life satisfaction. It encompasses a broad spectrum, ranging from hedonia, which focuses on pleasure, fulfillment of needs, and pain-free existence, to eudaimonia, which emphasizes a meaningful life rooted in personal values and growth. This dichotomy distinguishes hedonia's focus on feelings and pleasurable experiences from eudaimonia's association with behavior and the pursuit of self-realization.

Well-being is a concept that has been debated for a long time, and it refers to both functioning well and feeling good.[23] It includes both material and non-material aspects. The academic debate surrounding well-being delves into discussions about its definition, measurement, and impact on the relationship between tourism development and residents. The evolution of well-being as a concept reflects a transition from a one-dimensional focus on income to a multi-dimensional understanding. It is initially dominated by materialistic ideas — the belief that money buys happiness — and the emphasis on income generation has shifted to income distribution. The basic needs approach recognizes inequality as fundamental and addresses questions about resource distribution, expanding the conceptualization of the good life beyond income to include health and education. This journey from a one-dimensional concept centered on income to a multi-dimensional understanding marks a significant evolution.

The concept of well-being is intricately tied to enhanced productivity and prolonged lifespans and comprises three discernible dimensions. The primary dimension is the material aspect, where income is a pivotal determinant. This material dimension underscores the significance of financial stability and resources in shaping an individual's overall well-being. The second dimension delves into the opportunities and choices available to individuals. This aligns with the capabilities approach, which

---

[23] For an excellent discussion about well-being, see Diener, E., Lucas, R., Schimmack, U. and Helliwell, J. (2009). *Well-Being for Public Policy*. New York: Oxford Academic, https://doi.org/10.1093/acprof:oso/9780195334074.001.0001, accessed 20 Dec. 2023.

emphasizes enabling individuals to pursue a life they value by expanding their capabilities. These expanded capabilities, in turn, translate into tangible life outcomes, thereby contributing to an individual's sense of well-being.

The third dimension is intimately tied to an individual's emotions and mindset regarding various facets of life. This emotional and psychological dimension encompasses mental health, satisfaction, and overall emotional well-being. Understanding and addressing these aspects are crucial for comprehensively gauging an individual's well-being. Despite the ongoing ambiguity surrounding the definition and measurement of well-being, the happiness literature consistently links it with the overarching concept of a good life.[24] This holistic perspective on well-being embraces elements beyond mere material wealth, encompassing purpose, positive relationships, autonomy, and social acceptance. The intricate interplay of these elements adds depth to the understanding of well-being, transcending a purely economic or quantifiable perspective.

Well-being, encompassing physical, mental, and emotional health, social connections, and life satisfaction, is a multifaceted concept often used broadly to include mental health, happiness, and physical health. Sen's perspective highlights that the availability of opportunities is essential for fulfilling capabilities and achieving well-being. It transcends a narrow focus on material aspects, recognizing the broader dimensions contributing to an individual's overall state of being. As researchers, policymakers, and practitioners engage in assessing well-being outcomes, considering opportunities emerges as a critical factor in comprehensively understanding and addressing the complexities of human welfare.

In tourism literature, the integration of well-being has become increasingly relevant. Travel and tourism, once predominantly associated with leisure and escapism, are now recognized as powerful contributors to individuals'

---

[24] For example, see Graham, C. (2009). *Happiness around the world. The paradox of happy peasants and miserable millionaires.* New York: Oxford University Press.

overall well-being. Travel experiences can provide opportunities for personal growth, cultural enrichment, and cultivating positive emotions. Moreover, the tourism industry can influence the material dimension of well-being by generating income and employment opportunities in destination communities. This economic impact, coupled with the social and cultural exchanges facilitated by tourism, contributes to the overall well-being of travelers and residents.

As the discourse on well-being in tourism expands, there is a growing acknowledgment of the need for sustainable and responsible tourism practices. Embracing such practices not only safeguards destinations' natural and cultural resources but also fosters a positive and fulfilling experience for all stakeholders involved. The multidimensional nature of well-being, encompassing material, opportunities, and emotional dimensions, provides a comprehensive framework for understanding an individual's quality of life. When applied to the context of tourism literature, this framework offers insights into the transformative potential of travel experiences and the symbiotic relationship between tourism and overall well-being. The ongoing exploration of these connections underscores the evolving landscape of well-being research and its diverse applications across various fields, including tourism's dynamic and ever-evolving realm.

Well-being and Opportunity

Opportunity, a versatile concept, finds its definition shaped by context but generally refers to a situation enabling someone to do something or achieve a specific goal. Within the realm of well-being, opportunity extends to the potential for individuals to fulfill their needs, wants, and aspirations. This encompasses diverse forms, including access to education, employment, healthcare, various resources, and participation in social and political systems. Social and economic mobility is closely intertwined with opportunities, allowing individuals to enhance their economic and social status. Socioeconomic status, race, gender, and location shape opportunities and influence well-being outcomes. In tourism, opportunities manifest in access to tourism resources, employment, and economic development, emphasizing their pivotal role in shaping individuals' lives and well-being.

Amartya Sen's conceptualization of opportunities underscores the multidimensional nature of human capabilities and the importance of enhancing individuals' freedom to pursue valuable opportunities. This approach highlights the intrinsic link between development and the expansion of human capabilities, encompassing material well-being and social, political, and cultural freedoms. Sen argues that traditional development measures, such as GDP per capita, must catch up in capturing the complexity of human well-being, advocating instead for a capabilities approach that focuses on promoting human flourishing and agency.

In Amartya Sen's capabilities approach, opportunities, achievements, and positional objectivity intersect to offer a comprehensive understanding of human development and well-being. Opportunities represent the choices available to individuals to pursue their goals and lead fulfilling lives, while achievements signify the tangible outcomes realized through these opportunities. Sen's concept of positional objectivity emphasizes evaluating well-being relative to individuals' aspirations rather than external benchmarks, highlighting the importance of subjective fulfillment over material wealth.

In tourism, opportunities abound through diverse experiences like cultural immersion, environmental exploration, and social interaction, enabling travelers to achieve personal goals and contribute to conservation efforts. By embracing positional objectivity, tourism destinations can prioritize travelers' subjective preferences and aspirations, fostering inclusive and fulfilling experiences that enhance human capabilities and promote sustainable development.

From a tourism perspective, Sen's framework emphasizes the need to provide travelers with meaningful experiences beyond mere consumption, considering their diverse capabilities and preferences for cultural immersion, environmental stewardship, and social engagement. For instance, tourism destinations facilitating authentic cultural exchanges, community-based initiatives, and sustainable practices align with Sen's approach by empowering tourists to engage with local communities, learn about different cultures, and contribute to positive social and environmental outcomes. In this way, tourism can play a pivotal role in enhancing human capabilities and fostering development that is inclusive, sustainable, and conducive to human flourishing.

Alternatively, tourism offers destination residents many economic, cultural, and community opportunities. Economically, tourism can catalyze job creation and entrepreneurial ventures, offering employment opportunities in various sectors. Culturally, residents can showcase their heritage through cultural events and markets, fostering a sense of pride and identity within the community. Furthermore, tourism can spur community development by supporting infrastructure projects and local initiatives, enhancing residents' quality of life. However, effective destination management is crucial to balance the benefits of tourism with potential challenges, ensuring sustainable development that prioritizes residents' well-being and preserves the destination's unique identity.

Sen defines opportunities in two key aspects: the availability of choices or outcomes a person can achieve and the choice process, which is the ability to control how these choices are made. Having a variety of options is important, but navigating and influencing the decision-making process is equally crucial. To effectively control the choice process, a person needs agentic capabilities. This means being able to evaluate different options, form preferences through self-reflection, and make decisions they can identify with and take responsibility for. These skills enable individuals to not only have choices but also to make meaningful and personally significant decisions.[25]

---

[25] Sen makes this distinction in various places (For example, Sen 1985: 209-12, 1999: 17-18, 37-41). See Sen A. (1985), Goals, commitment, and identity", *The Journal of Law, Economics, and Organization*, Vol. 1 No. 2, pp. 341-355; and Sen, A. (1999). *Development as freedom*. Oxford University Press.

For example, residents in tourism-rich areas have various opportunities that can significantly improve their quality of life. These opportunities can be understood through two main aspects: the availability of choices or outcomes and the choice process. A resident might have the opportunity to start a bed-and-breakfast, offer guided tours, or sell handmade crafts to tourists. These options represent the different outcomes a resident can achieve. However, it is not just about having choices; it is also about being able to control how these choices are made. This control involves assessing different options, forming preferences, and making decisions that align with their values and interests.

Consider a coastal town that is undergoing rapid tourism development. On the surface, the influx of tourists brings structural opportunities such as new jobs, increased income, and improved infrastructure, representing substantial capability inputs. However, the ability of residents to convert these inputs into actual well-being varies significantly due to situational factors. For example, Maria, a local shop owner, benefits from the increased tourist traffic, which boosts her sales and allows her to expand her business. She has both the agency freedom and the agency achievement to enhance her well-being.

In contrast, John, a lifelong fisherman, finds that the tourism boom disrupts his traditional way of life. Increased cruise and boat traffic and coastal development harm fish populations, making it harder for him to sustain his livelihood. Despite having the structural opportunities to transition into a tourism-related job, John lacks the necessary skills and education. Additionally, his deep connection to fishing as a way of life means that shifting to a new occupation would not align with his valued goals. In this case, John has agency freedom (the theoretical ability to pursue a new job) but lacks agency achievement (realizing a fulfilling new career). His situational factors, such as environmental changes and skill deficits, create a gap between his freedom and achievement.

Moreover, the influx of tourists leads to increased living costs, making it difficult for lower-income residents to maintain their standard of living. While tourism brings economic growth, the benefits are unevenly distributed, and some community members experience diminished well-being due to rising prices and environmental degradation. This scenario illustrates how vulnerability contexts, such as economic disparities and environmental impacts, can hinder the effective use of structural opportunities and personal resources, leading to a discrepancy between capability inputs and agency achievement.

Sen's work emphasizes that having structural opportunities and personal resources doesn't guarantee an individual's ability to use them effectively, as situational factors can significantly impact one's agency capacity. He distinguishes between "capability inputs" (the total set of personal and structural resources) and two types of agency: "agency freedom," the freedom to pursue valued goals, and "agency achievement," the actual realization of those goals. The gap between freedom and achievement often arises due to situational factors that align closely with various vulnerability contexts.

Theoretical Foundations of Well-being

At the outset of my career as an applied economist, I emphasized the material underpinnings of well-being, quantifying it through parameters such as income and caloric intake, encapsulating the physical dimension of well-being. However, it is crucial to underscore that well-being extends beyond the tangible, material aspects and incorporates the opportunities accessible to individuals and their capacity to actualize them. Furthermore, it is equally imperative to consider individuals' sentiments regarding these opportunities and their realization. In essence, well-being emerges as a nuanced and multi-faceted concept, encompassing material and non-material facets and elucidating their interconnectedness. Moving forward, I will explore four pivotal theoretical frameworks that intricately address well-being within the context of tourism literature.

Utility Theory (UT)

When considering theoretical frameworks for understanding the relationship between tourism and well-being, utility theory emerges as a pertinent approach. This theoretical lens delves into individuals' decision-making processes, focusing on preferences and feelings and how these can be satisfied through goods, services, or income. In the context of tourism and residents' well-being, utility theory can offer insights into how tourism development impacts people's preferences and feelings. For instance, tourism development may provide increased income opportunities or access to valued goods and services, ultimately contributing to improved well-being. Furthermore, utility theory aids in understanding how residents' preferences and feelings towards tourism evolve as they adapt to its presence in their community.

With its foundation in maximizing satisfaction, utility theory sheds light on how travel experiences significantly contribute to overall well-being. As travelers seek destinations, activities, and experiences per their preferences, the theory guides decision-making processes within tourism development. Going beyond the economic aspect, utility theory recognizes the experiential dimensions of travel, acknowledging their impact on non-material aspects of well-being. For instance, Kucukusta and Guillet[26] applied utility theory to people's choices and preferences by analyzing spa visitors' preferences. Examining benefit scores related to various product preferences revealed insights into consumer choices, providing valuable implications for enhancing tourism experiences. By delving into benefit scores associated with multiple product preferences, the analysis directly aligns with utility theory, which elucidates how individuals choose to maximize their overall satisfaction or well-being.

In consumer decision-making for tourism experiences, these benefit scores serve as tangible representations of the subjective utility consumers

---

[26] Kucukusta D., Guillet B.D. (2014). Measuring spa-goers' preferences: A conjoint analysis approach. *International Journal of Hospitality Management.* 41, 115–124.

attribute to different products. The subjective nature of utility, as emphasized in utility theory, is mirrored in the diverse preferences uncovered by examining these scores. Essentially, the insights derived from this analysis illuminate consumers' intricate decision-making process and offer businesses and tourism providers a roadmap for improving their offerings. By tailoring products and services to align with the identified preferences, there lies a significant potential for enhancing the overall tourism experience and, consequently, elevating customer satisfaction — a core objective in both utility theory and consumer-oriented businesses.

However, concerns arise regarding the comprehensive explanatory power of utility theory in this context. While it can illuminate how tourism development influences preferences and feelings, the theory needs to capture the complexity of the relationship between tourism and well-being. Its assumption that people's preferences and feelings are stable and consistent is challenged by the dynamic nature of reality, where these factors may change over time and be influenced by cultural, social, and emotional elements. Moreover, utility theory neglects to consider power dynamics and structural factors that may shape the distribution of benefits and costs in tourism development. Additionally, the theory overlooks the long-term effects of tourism development on residents' well-being.

In the tourism literature, utility theory has been applied to analyze residents' well-being in areas affected by tourism. The theory posits that individuals strive to maximize their utility or satisfaction by making choices aligned with their preferences for goods and services.[27] Researchers have utilized utility theory to investigate how various tourism-related factors, such as increased noise, traffic, and crowding, impact residents' well-being. Notably, this framework highlights the importance of residents' perceptions in shaping their well-being. For instance, a resident's well-being may not be negatively affected by increased noise from tourism if

---

[27] See, for example, Bimonte, S. (2022). Happiness and Tourism Activities: An Empirical and Theoretical interpretation. In Croes, R. & Yang, Y. (2022). (eds.) *A modern guide to tourism economics.* Edward Elgar Publishing: Cheltenham, UK, p. 259-276.

they perceive it as stemming from a desirable form of tourism, such as a concert.

As I explore the potential of utility theory in understanding the interplay between tourism and well-being, it becomes evident that while the framework offers valuable insights, it could be more comprehensive in its explanatory capacity. The theory's static assumption about stable preferences and feelings and oversight of broader contextual factors, such as access to resources, availability, quality infrastructure, and culture, underscores the necessity of complementing it with other theories and frameworks. A holistic understanding of the relationship between tourism development and residents' well-being requires a comprehensive approach considering dynamic factors, power dynamics, structural influences, and evolving perceptions over time.

Social Exchange Theory (SET)

This leads me to the next aspect of my research: the theoretical frameworks that inform my approach to understanding well-being. One such framework is the social exchange theory, which provides a structured blueprint for analyzing problems.[28] Social Exchange Theory offers valuable insights into how positive interactions contribute to the well-being of communities, particularly in the context of cultural exchange between tourists and hosts. By examining these exchanges through the lens of SET, we gain a deeper understanding of cultural well-being and the mutual benefits of cultural interactions. Additionally, SET sheds light on the dynamics of tourist satisfaction, emphasizing the significance of meeting expectations and fulfilling experiences in enhancing overall well-being.

According to this theory, one should begin by examining the activity itself. In the context of my research, this refers to tourism development. Next,

---

[28] See, for example, Nunkoo, R., & So, K. K. F. (2016). Residents' support for tourism: Testing alternative structural models. *Journal of travel research*, 55(7), 847-861.

attention is given to the benefits generated by this activity. Subsequently, it becomes vital to identify who receives these benefits and who does not. Based on this analysis, predictions can be made regarding the support and engagement of those who benefit from tourism development.

Translating this theory to the context of tourism, I examined tourism development as an activity and explored the potential benefits it can bring. By identifying the individuals or groups that benefit from tourism, I can predict their level of support for its development. This approach provides a foundation for understanding the dynamics between well-being and tourism and the motivations and interests of various stakeholders. The social exchange theory is a valuable framework for understanding the dynamics between tourism development and residents' well-being. This theory systematically outlines the relationship between variables by identifying the activity — in this case, tourism development — and then analyzing its benefits. Applied to tourism, this framework allows for a structured examination of how tourism impacts residents' well-being.

In my initial research, I leveraged the social exchange theory to scrutinize the impact of tourism development on residents' well-being. By treating tourism development as an activity and analyzing the associated benefits, I predicted which individuals or groups would support it. However, it is crucial to acknowledge the theory's inherent limitations. For example, the social exchange theory, rooted in the assumption of rational self-interest, does not account for the complexity of human decision-making influenced by emotions, social norms, and culture. Furthermore, it lacks consideration for power dynamics and structural factors that may shape tourism development's distribution of benefits and costs. The theory's static nature also fails to explain dynamic relationships and long-term effects.

Applying Social Exchange Theory (SET) to the realm of well-being in tourism literature unveils insightful perspectives on the intricate dynamics between tourists and destination communities. As an economist initially focused on the material foundations of well-being — measuring it through income and caloric metrics — the lens of SET adds a crucial social dimension to the analysis. In the context of tourist-host interactions, SET illuminates the reciprocal relationships where positive cultural exchanges and mutual understanding contribute to both parties' emotional and psychological well-being. The theory's emphasis on trust and cooperation underscores their pivotal roles in shaping positive interactions. Moreover, SET proves instrumental in examining the economic impact of tourism, revealing how income generation and employment opportunities positively affect the material well-being of local populations.

By delving into social capital, SET further demonstrates how positive exchanges enhance the overall well-being of communities. Cultural well-being, influenced by the exchange of cultures between tourists and hosts, gains deeper insights through SET's perspective. The theory also proves valuable in understanding tourist satisfaction, emphasizing the role of expectations and their fulfillment in shaping overall well-being.[29] In the context of sustainability, SET encourages a long-term view of relationships, promoting strategies that balance rewards and costs for tourists and local communities. Applying SET to the tourism industry provides a comprehensive understanding of social exchanges, contributing to developing strategies that foster positive interactions and sustainable practices, thereby enhancing the collective well-being of all involved stakeholders.

While the social exchange theory provides a useful framework for understanding the relationship between tourism development and residents' well-being, it has inherent limitations. The assumption that individuals act solely based on rational self-interest overlooks the multifaceted nature of human decision-making, influenced by emotions, social norms, and cultural nuances. Moreover, the theory's failure to consider power dynamics and structural factors may limit its

---

[29] See, for example, Moyle, B., Croy, G. and Weiler, B. (2010). Tourism interaction on islands: the community and visitor social exchange. *International Journal of Culture Tourism and Hospitality Research*, 4(2), 97-107.

applicability in explaining the distribution of benefits and costs in tourism development. Recognizing these limitations, it becomes evident that the social exchange theory, while insightful, should be complemented by other theories and frameworks and coupled with observational data for a more comprehensive understanding.

It is essential to note that the social exchange theory, operating on rational self-interest, may only encompass some aspects of residents' responses to tourism development and their overall well-being. Many factors influence human behavior, including emotions, empathy, and cultural intricacies. Therefore, while the theory provides a foundation, it cannot be the sole determinant in explaining the complexities of the relationship between tourism development and well-being.

Human Development (HD)

The concept of human development and capability presents a distinctive blueprint for approaching the question of well-being. Unlike the sequential social exchange theory approach, the human development blueprint incorporates inputs, outputs, and conversion factors, providing a comprehensive understanding of the steps and methods needed. Amartya Sen's capability approach, a cornerstone of this framework, emphasizes that individuals should have access to a wide range of opportunities for a high level of well-being. This approach extends beyond traditional measures of income or wealth, focusing on capabilities and opportunities, including the ability to lead a healthy life, access education, and participate in the political process.

The capability approach diverges from conventional assessments by evaluating individuals based on their achievement of essential outcomes and exploring the practical opportunities at their disposal. It underscores the importance of distinguishing between agency — the capacity for autonomous decision-making — and opportunity — the existence of feasible choices. Essential factors influencing capability include access to goods and services, purchasing power, personal constraints, societal norms, discrimination, and environmental obstacles. By examining these intricate facets, the capability approach provides a richer comprehension of individuals' capabilities and the intricate socio-economic dynamics influencing their potential for personal development and well-being.

Sen's departure from conventional utility theories lies in his recognition of the limitations of assessing well-being solely through utility. Instead, he proposes a more comprehensive approach, defining well-being as an individual's "ability to do valuable acts or reach valuable states of being," termed "functionings." These encompass the various activities and conditions a person can achieve. Furthermore, Sen introduces the concept of "capability," reflecting the range of functionings a person can attain and choose from. For instance, a person's well-being is not merely measured by their achievements but also by the opportunities they have had to pursue. Sen's framework extends beyond traditional economic perspectives by considering allocating societal resources to enhance the quality of life. This approach acknowledges that many factors, such as age, gender, sociocultural background, and personal circumstances, influence the collection of valued functionings and perceived capabilities. Thus, Sen's analysis emphasizes the importance of understanding the complex interplay between individual capabilities and socio-environmental factors in assessing well-being.

The Capability Approach (CA) was initially conceptualized as a framework for evaluating and quantifying individuals' "capability" or freedom to pursue and achieve the "functionings" they value, extending beyond mere economic resources. Rather than focusing solely on material wealth or happiness as a mental state, the CA emphasizes individuals' ability to engage in valued activities and states of being. "Functionings" encompass what individuals can accomplish with their available resources. At the same time, "capability" represents the range of achieved and achievable opportunities individuals value and have reason to value. To realize capability, individuals convert economic resources through three key conversion factors: the "personal conversion factor," involving physical condition, intelligence, and personal traits; the "social conversion factor," influenced by social norms, status, and public policies; and the "environmental conversion factor" encompassing factors like climate, geography, and infrastructure. Through this lens, the CA provides a nuanced understanding of human well-being by considering the dynamic interplay between resources, opportunities, and individual capabilities within various socio-environmental contexts.[30]

The conversion factors highlighted in the human development blueprint are instrumental in transforming inputs into outputs. Often referred to as throughput factors, these elements include institutions, policies, social norms, culture, and technology. They are not inputs or outputs themselves, but they shape the transformation process. For instance, education and healthcare may be inputs in human development, while improved living standards and well-being may be outputs. Conversion factors like good governance and effective policies ensure that inputs lead to desired outputs. It is essential to note that these factors can have positive or negative impacts on outcomes, such as how governance affects resource utilization efficiency or how cultural norms influence education outcomes.

In the context of tourism and its impact on residents' well-being, conversion factors play a pivotal role in determining how tourism inputs are transformed into outputs. Policies and regulations, effective governance, and community involvement are among the conversion factors influencing the relationship between tourism development and residents' well-being. For example, the CA offers a robust framework for analyzing indigenous tourism dynamics. Central to this approach is the recognition of human agency and empowerment, which are vital for individuals to pursue lives of value within their unique cultural contexts. Indigenous traditions share this emphasis on context-specific well-being and participatory decision-making processes, aligning closely

---

[30] See, for example, Croes, R. (2012). Assessing tourism development from Sen's capability approach. *Journal of Travel Research, 51*(5), 542-554.

with the CA's principles. By embracing cultural diversity and community involvement, Sen's framework resonates with Indigenous values, fostering interdisciplinary collaboration to honor Indigenous perspectives and promote human development. In Indigenous tourism, this convergence facilitates preserving and celebrating Indigenous cultures, languages, and traditions, bolstering communities' capabilities to lead culturally vibrant lives. However, this endeavor necessitates adherence to principles of inclusivity and respect for indigenous knowledge systems to ensure meaningful engagement. Moreover, the Capability Approach underscores the importance of environmental sustainability, urging eco-conscious practices to safeguard natural resources and enhance human well-being through indigenous tourism initiatives.

The capability approach finds application in tourism literature, offering insights into how tourism affects individuals and communities. Studies analyzing the impact of tourism on fishing communities and residents in destinations have used the capability approach to understand the effects on livelihoods and overall well-being. This approach considers access to public services, social capital, and community cohesion, providing a more nuanced understanding of the impact beyond material goods or income. It emphasizes the importance of focusing on the ability to pursue what individuals value, making it a valuable theoretical framework for understanding the complex dynamics of tourism and well-being.

In my research, examining conversion factors has proven to be a central component, providing valuable insights into the intricate connections between tourism development and well-being. This nuanced comprehension is demonstrated by applying diverse conversion factors across various dimensions. For instance, in the economic context, the critical conversion factor between tourism revenue and employment has played a pivotal role in understanding how financial gains generated by tourism contribute to local job opportunities, thereby shedding light on the community's economic well-being. Additionally, a cultural conversion factor has been implemented to quantify the influence of tourism on the preservation of cultural heritage, establishing a link between tourism activities and the cultural sustainability aspect of well-being.

Moreover, using a social conversion factor assesses the impact of tourism on community engagement by investigating the correlation between tourist numbers and local participation in activities, thus revealing insights into the community's social cohesion and overall well-being. Additionally, a health-related conversion factor evaluates the influence of tourism development on healthcare accessibility for residents, demonstrating the interconnected nature between tourism revenue and the health and well-being of the population. These conversion factors offer theoretical elucidations and anchor the interpretation of findings in empirical evidence, recognizing the influential roles of mediators and moderators in addressing previously confounding inconsistencies. This approach contributes to a holistic understanding of the intricate relationships between tourism development and well-being, underscoring the importance of contextual nuances in shaping these dynamics.

In each of these examples, the conversion factors are crucial in understanding the intricate relationships between tourism development and various dimensions of well-being. They provide a quantitative basis for evaluating the impacts and outcomes, allowing for a more nuanced interpretation of results grounded in both theoretical frameworks and empirical evidence. Recognizing mediators and moderators further enhances the analysis, addressing inconsistencies in results and contributing to a more comprehensive understanding of the complex interplay between tourism development and well-being in diverse contexts.

Context is critical in theory building and understanding, as it provides the necessary background information and conditions that shape the relationship between variables. We need to consider context to ensure our understanding of a phenomenon is sufficient, leading to consistency in results. Acknowledging context helps bridge the gap between theory and real-world applications, providing a more nuanced and comprehensive

understanding of the intricate relationships within the human development
and capability framework.

Subjective Well-being (SW)

Subjective well-being introduces a paradigm shift in our understanding
of individual prosperity, challenging traditional measures by emphasizing
the significance of personal evaluations in assessing life conditions and
opportunities. At its core, subjective well-being asserts that individuals
are the best judges of their happiness, arguing that external metrics may
not capture the full spectrum of their satisfaction or contentment. This
perspective recognizes the complexity of human experiences, suggesting
that objective factors like income or societal norms do not solely determine
one's well-being.[31]

An intriguing aspect of subjective well-being lies in the potential
disjunction between objective circumstances and personal satisfaction.
It is common for individuals facing seemingly unfavorable conditions,
such as below-average incomes, to rate their well-being as remarkably
high. This dissonance highlights the importance of considering individual
perceptions and feelings when evaluating the overall quality of life. For
example, in the context of tourism development, subjective well-being
plays a crucial role. Tourism has the potential to shape individuals' life
experiences by introducing new perspectives, cultures, and opportunities
for personal growth. It goes beyond economic considerations, assessing
realms of cultural exposure and the overall enrichment of life experiences.
Therefore, tourism's impact on subjective well-being cannot be measured

---

[31] The recently edited book by Uysal and Sirgy offers comprehensive and thought-
provoking discussions on the perspectives of subjective well-being in the context
of tourism. This volume delves into the intricate relationship between tourism
experiences and the subjective well-being of travelers, exploring various theoretical
frameworks, empirical research, and practical applications. See Uysal, M. and Sirgy,
M.J. (eds.) *Handbook of Tourism and Quality of life Research II*. Cham, Switzerland:
Springer.

solely by economic indicators; it should also consider its ability to enhance individuals' happiness and satisfaction.

Consider how each resident perceives tourism development. Their perception is intrinsically linked to their sense of well-being, creating a complex relationship deeply rooted in individual experiences. Traditional measures of well-being, such as income and employment, are often used to evaluate the impact of tourism development. However, these objective variables can lead to different experiences for different people. Therefore, relying solely on an objective list of conditions to assess well-being can result in significant misinterpretations of a person's well-being.

Take, for example, a coastal town that has recently experienced a surge in tourism development. The local government and developers highlight the benefits of increased income and job opportunities, traditionally seen as indicators of improved well-being. However, residents' perceptions of these changes can vary widely, illustrating the complexity of the relationship between tourism development and well-being.

For instance, a local shop owner, Maria, perceives the influx of tourists as a boon. Her sales have increased significantly, allowing her to expand her business and improve her family's financial stability. From her perspective, tourism development has enhanced her well-being by providing economic benefits and a sense of security.

In contrast, John, a lifelong resident and fisherman, experiences tourism development differently. The increased boat traffic and coastal construction disrupt his fishing activities, making it harder for him to sustain his livelihood. Additionally, the town's once peaceful atmosphere has become noisy and crowded, which John finds distressing. Despite the objective indicators of economic growth, John's well-being has declined due to the negative impact on his daily life and work.

These examples highlight the limitations of using objective measures alone to assess well-being. While the town's overall income and job opportunities may have improved, the subjective experiences of residents like John reveal a more nuanced picture. By incorporating subjective measures, such as personal satisfaction and happiness, policymakers can better understand and address the diverse impacts of tourism development on residents' well-being.

Recognizing these subjective experiences allows for more tailored and empathetic approaches to tourism development. For instance, creating designated fishing zones or implementing noise control measures could help mitigate the adverse effects on residents like John. This approach improves individual well-being and fosters a more balanced and sustainable development strategy that benefits the entire community.

The call for self-assessment in measuring subjective happiness represents a significant paradigm shift compared to conventional societal benchmarks. Instead of relying on external criteria or expert constructs, this approach places faith in individuals' abilities to accurately evaluate and express their sense of fulfillment. It implies that well-being is a deeply personal and subjective experience transcending standardized measures. In the societal context, this subjective stance challenges traditional views on happiness and suggests that a person's life experience may not necessarily align with objective indicators. This shift in perspective prompts a reevaluation of societal norms and expectations, emphasizing the importance of individual autonomy in determining what constitutes a satisfying and fulfilling life.

The application of subjective well-being becomes particularly crucial in tourism development. Understanding how tourism shapes individuals' life experiences provides valuable insights into the intricate relationship between leisure activities and subjective happiness. With its potential to introduce new perspectives, cultures, and experiences, tourism becomes a dynamic force influencing subjective well-being.

Tourism's impact on subjective well-being goes beyond economic considerations, delving into personal growth, cultural exposure, and the overall enrichment of life experiences. The subjective well-being lens suggests that the success of tourism development should not be solely measured by economic indicators but also by its ability to enhance individuals' happiness and satisfaction. This approach challenges conventional wisdom by asserting that individuals are the ultimate authorities on their happiness. It prompts a reevaluation of societal norms and has profound implications for understanding the impact of phenomena like tourism on individuals' overall life experiences. Embracing the subjective stance offers a more nuanced and comprehensive understanding of well-being, acknowledging the diversity and subjectivity inherent in the human experience.[32]

The Broadening Concept of the Human Welfare Paradigm

The human welfare paradigm stands as a holistic perspective on development and social policy, prioritizing the well-being of individuals and communities. Central to this approach is the focus on improving living conditions and meeting the basic needs of all people, encompassing fundamental necessities like access to food, shelter, healthcare, and education. In tandem, the human welfare paradigm strongly emphasizes social and economic rights, acknowledging the right to work, the right to form trade unions, and the right to social security.

Diverging from other development paradigms, such as the growth paradigm that views human welfare as an outcome of economic development, this paradigm contends that economic growth alone is insufficient for ensuring well-being. It advocates for a more comprehensive approach

---

[32] Please see my editorial in Journal of Destination Management and Marketing, Croes, R. (2016). Connecting tourism development with small island destinations and with the well-being of the island residents. *Journal of Destination Marketing & Management*, 5(1), 1-4.

to address the intricate social, economic, and environmental challenges facing communities today.

The human welfare paradigm aligns harmoniously with the concept of human development, championing the expansion of people's capabilities and opportunities. Mirroring its principles are the Sustainable Development Goals (SDGs), established by the United Nations in 2015, which aim to eradicate poverty, protect the environment, and ensure universal peace and prosperity. By harnessing the potential of tourism as a driver of positive change, stakeholders can advance various Sustainable Development Goals (4SDGs), such as promoting decent work and economic growth, fostering responsible consumption and production, combating climate change, and conserving terrestrial ecosystems and biodiversity. Initiatives aimed at empowering local communities, promoting cultural preservation, and implementing sustainable tourism practices contribute to economic prosperity and foster social inclusivity and environmental stewardship. Moreover, the transformative power of tourism lies in its capacity to inspire cross-sectoral collaborations, innovative solutions, and inclusive development pathways, making it a potent force for realizing the vision of a more equitable, resilient, and sustainable world.

At its core, the human welfare paradigm asserts that all individuals have the right to a decent standard of living, with governments and societies bearing the responsibility to fulfill everyone's basic needs. In the realm of tourism literature, the human welfare paradigm becomes a critical lens through which to examine the impacts of tourism on local communities. It advocates for socially and economically sustainable tourism development, recognizing that tourism can positively and negatively influence localities. A pivotal concept in this discourse is "pro-poor tourism," which strives to ensure that tourism benefits the poorest and most marginalized members of society. Emphasizing community involvement in planning and management, this approach aims to guarantee fair distribution of benefits.

Similarly, "community-based tourism" aligns with the human welfare paradigm, presenting tourism as a tool for empowering local communities and enhancing their well-being. The approach underscores the importance of close collaboration with local communities to develop tourism offerings that meet their needs and priorities. Critics, however, argue about the practical challenges and limitations of implementing such approaches, suggesting the need for integration with other development strategies.

When not conscientiously managed, tourism development can lead to displacement, cultural erosion, and environmental degradation, exacerbating social and economic inequalities. The human welfare paradigm in tourism literature accentuates the imperative to ensure that tourism benefits are equitably shared and minimize negative impacts. It places a premium on inclusive approaches like pro-poor and community-based tourism, urging a collective commitment to prioritize the well-being of residents.

Pro-poor tourism, a focal point in tourism literature, embodies the principles of the human welfare paradigm. It operates on the premise that tourism can be a potent tool for poverty reduction and community well-being if planned and managed inclusively. The principles of beneficiary participation and income generation play central roles, aiming to involve local communities in decision-making and create economic opportunities for them.

In tandem, community-based tourism (CBT) emerges as a nuanced strategy within the human welfare paradigm, stressing the importance of involving local communities in the planning and managing of tourism activities. Adopting a "bottom-up" development approach, CBT begins with the needs and priorities of local communities, allowing them to take ownership of the tourism development process. Although critics highlight challenges in its implementation, both pro-poor tourism and CBT resonate with the human welfare paradigm's core tenets.

The human welfare paradigm in tourism literature advocates for socially and economically sustainable tourism development. It strongly emphasizes pro-poor and community-based tourism, underscoring the need for inclusive approaches that prioritize the well-being of local communities. Despite challenges and criticisms, these paradigms offer valuable insights into fostering equitable tourism development and combatting poverty, aligning with the broader principles of the human welfare perspective. Several of my studies adhere to the paradigm's principles of human development, poverty, agency, equity, and governance.[33]

Foundational Frameworks in Shaping My Research on Tourism Development

My research paradigm shifted when I made a conscious decision to move beyond the narrow confines of rationality and self-interest when exploring the intricate relationship between tourism development and well-being. Realizing the limitations of traditional utility theories, which predominantly focus on individual preferences and satisfaction, I embraced a more holistic perspective anchored in human development and capability.

The human development framework, unlike linear models, introduced a cyclical process involving inputs, conversion factors, and outcomes. It highlighted the significance of various inputs in overall well-being, such as education, healthcare, income, and freedom. The conversion factors, including social interactions, policies, and cultural influences, played a pivotal role in determining how these inputs translated into capabilities, ultimately influencing the ability to lead a fulfilling life.

This broader lens allowed me to delve into the complexities of the relationship between tourism development and human development.

---

[33] See, for example, Croes, R., Kubickova, M. & Ridderstaat, J. (2022). Destination competitiveness and human development: the compelling critical force of human agency. *Journal of Hospitality and Tourism Research*, https://doi.org/10.1177/10963480221140022.

Acknowledging the multifaceted nature of well-being, the research extended beyond immediate impacts on individuals to consider broader societal implications and long-term outcomes. The recognition of conversion factors became crucial, emphasizing this relationship's nonlinear and context-dependent nature.

As I immersed myself in this exploration, the capability approach emerged as a promising framework. It highlighted the individual's ability to achieve valuable "beings and doings" in life as a measure of well-being, emphasizing the importance of life experiences in understanding one's overall quality of life. This approach introduced the concept of "functionings," encompassing objective aspects like health and education and subjective experiences like happiness and autonomy.

A pivotal turning point in my research came with the realization that life experiences are central to comprehending well-being, surpassing the limitations of traditional measures such as GDP per capita. This insight resonates with the influential Stiglitz Report, formally titled "Report by the Commission on the Measurement of Economic Performance and Social Progress."[34] Commissioned in 2008, the report, led by Nobel laureate economists Joseph Stiglitz, Amartya Sen, and Jean-Paul Fitoussi, addressed the need for more economic indicators in measuring societal well-being. The report underscored the necessity of a combined approach that considers objective and subjective measures to provide a more accurate representation of well-being, aligning with the crux of my research that emphasizes the significance of life experiences in understanding overall satisfaction and quality of life.

Incorporating insights from the Stiglitz Report, my research aimed to balance subjective perceptions and objective indicators. This nuanced measurement approach allowed for a comprehensive evaluation of

---

[34] Stiglitz, J.M., Sen, A. & Fitoussi, J. (2009). *Report by the commission on the measurement of economic performance and social progress.* Paris: Commission on the measurement of economic performance and social progress. Retrieved January 6, 2024 from http://www.stiglitz-sen-fitoussi.fr/documents/rapport_anglais.pdf.

tourism's impacts on different dimensions of well-being. The debate on objective versus subjective indicators in the broader literature on quality of life further reinforced the importance of considering individual perceptions, aligning with the argument that quality of life is inherently subjective and should be measured through open-ended surveys.

Incorporating the capability approach into my research marked a significant departure from traditional economic theories that often prioritize material aspects in assessing development and well-being. The capability approach, championed by Amartya Sen and Martha Nussbaum, broadens the scope beyond GDP-centric measures and emphasizes the inherent diversity in individuals' abilities to lead fulfilling lives. This diversity is intricately tied to the social, economic, and political environments that shape individuals' capabilities.

My research revolves around these two key dimensions: material foundations and opportunities and the subjective assessment of well-being. Notably, my research primarily centers on the residents of destinations, recognizing that the well-being of tourists is an equally significant aspect that can be explored separately within the quality of life and well-being research.[35] The concept of "functionings" within the capability approach underscores the importance of considering various aspects contributing to human well-being. These can include basic needs such as health and education and more intangible and subjective elements like autonomy, social connections, and a sense of purpose. By recognizing the multifaceted nature of human experiences, the capability approach provides a framework for acknowledging the richness and variety of individual lives, thus contributing to a more comprehensive understanding of well-being.

Moreover, the cyclical nature of the human development framework, with its inputs, conversion factors, and outcomes, introduces a dynamic

---

[35] See, for example, Uysal, M., Sirgy, M. J., Woo, E., & Kim, H. (L.). (2016). Quality of life (QOL) and well-being research in tourism. *Tourism Management, 53,* 244–261. https://doi.org/10.1016/j.tourman.2015.07.013.

dimension to the analysis. This acknowledges that the relationship between tourism development and well-being is not static but evolves, influenced by many factors. The conversion factors, in particular, highlight the role of social interactions, policies, and cultural influences in mediating the impact of tourism on well-being. This dynamic perspective is crucial in capturing the complexity and context-specific nature of the relationship.

As the research unfolded, it became increasingly apparent that the measurement of well-being is a complex and nuanced task. As highlighted by the Stiglitz Report, the debate between objective and subjective indicators introduced a critical dimension to this challenge. Objective measures, such as GDP per capita, provide a quantitative snapshot but may need to capture the intricacies of individual experiences. On the other hand, subjective measures, derived from individual perceptions and experiences, offer a more personal and qualitative understanding of well-being. The fusion of both approaches, as the Stiglitz Report advocates, enables a more holistic evaluation that considers both the tangible and intangible aspects of human flourishing.

Context matters emerged as a central theme in the research journey. The understanding that the relationship between tourism development and well-being is contingent on specific conditions challenges the traditional inclination towards generalization. Recognizing the role of mediators and moderators within specific contexts emphasizes the need for a nuanced, context-dependent approach. This shift from a rigid theoretical framework to an appreciation of contextual intricacies allows for a more realistic and applicable analysis of the impacts of tourism on human development and capability.

My research trajectory underwent a paradigm shift, evolving from reductionist perspectives to embracing a more comprehensive, dynamic, and context-sensitive approach. By integrating the capability approach, human development framework, and insights from the Stiglitz Report, the study sought to contribute a richer understanding of how tourism development shapes the diverse dimensions of human well-being. This journey represented a progression from rigid rationality to a more holistic, human-centric approach, aiming for a more inclusive and meaningful assessment of societal progress. In conclusion, informed by the ongoing discourse on well-being measurement, my research aimed to offer a nuanced understanding of the intricate interplay between tourism development and the diverse dimensions of human well-being, encapsulating a transformative shift in perspective.

Are People Happy

In the opening of this chapter, it is crucial to confront a pivotal question that forms the basis for our exploration into the intricate interplay between tourism and well-being: Is human happiness an inherent trait? Throughout civilization, individuals have grappled with the concept of well-being, contemplating the optimal ways to exist and thrive. Thoroughly examining this inquiry becomes essential before discussing the potential correlations between tourism and well-being. After all, ascertaining whether tourism can genuinely enhance well-being would only be possible by establishing a foundational understanding of individual happiness.

Aristotle delineates two categories of happiness: hedonia and eudaimonia. Hedonia encompasses positive feelings, life evaluations, and positive emotions, constituting a sense of feeling good in and about life on both affective and cognitive levels. Feeling good in life encompasses the immediate, momentary sources of pleasure and contentment derived from day-to-day experiences, such as enjoying a delicious meal or spending time with loved ones. On the other hand, eudaimonia encompasses a more profound and lasting sense of contentment with life arising from overarching life circumstances, accomplishments, and values. This comprehensive viewpoint considers enduring elements such as personal and professional achievements, meaningful relationships, and a sense of purpose. Both dimensions contribute to overall well-being, with the former rooted in immediate joys and the latter in a deeper, more sustained contentment derived from the overall quality and direction of one's life. In Aristotle's perspective, this dichotomy serves as a valuable framework for comprehending the nuanced dimensions of happiness and lays a foundation for exploring its potential intersections with tourism.

Grasping Happiness

This critical introduction underscores the necessity of grasping the foundational essence of human happiness before embarking on a meaningful exploration. A thorough comprehension of the constituents that contribute to happiness is deemed essential, serving as a prerequisite for any subsequent inquiry into the potential impact of tourism on well-being. Without this contextual foundation, an investigation into how tourism might influence happiness lacks a crucial framework. The inquiry questions the effectiveness of tourism as a catalyst for happiness if individuals are not inherently happy, as external interventions may prove ineffectual. Considering the primal objective of fostering happiness, aligned with the American Declaration of Independence's pursuit of happiness, it becomes imperative to navigate the complexities of human happiness before delving into potential intersections with the tourism domain.

Exploring the dynamics of human happiness involves not only examining it but also considering the complexities of its temporal stability and vulnerability to external influences. One dimension of this multifaceted investigation centers around set points, asserting that an individual's happiness is intricately linked to their inherent personality traits. This implies that each person possesses a unique baseline of happiness that acts as a stable point around which their emotional well-being revolves. On a parallel track, the exploration introduces the intriguing notion of the 'hedonic treadmill.' This concept posits that any sudden spikes in happiness, often triggered by external events like winning the lottery, are transient.

Despite the initial excitement, people often acclimate to these alterations, and their happiness levels ultimately return to the predetermined baseline.

Essentially, the hedonic treadmill questions the endurance of externally triggered joy, indicating that the lasting effect on overall happiness is constrained. This is due to our inherent tendency to adapt to such changes, making us only as content as we were initially. For instance, consider the euphoria experienced by a lottery winner. Initially, the newfound wealth and opportunities may elevate their happiness, but as time progresses, the initial elation wanes, and the individual returns to their pre-windfall state of happiness.

This recurring pattern underscores the resilience of our innate happiness baseline and how temporary factors impact our long-term well-being. However, suppose interventions consistently guide happiness to this baseline through personal growth. In that case, it suggests that even in challenging circumstances, individuals could achieve similar happiness levels as those in more favorable conditions. Take Paraguay, for example, where, despite economic struggles, 85 percent of residents rank high on a positive emotions index, according to the latest Gallup poll on well-being. This challenges our assumptions about the link between wealth and happiness, raising doubts about the efficacy of policy interventions.

However, when considering the context of stable happiness baselines, an important subtlety becomes apparent — individuals exhibit variability in their baseline happiness levels. This divergence can be ascribed to many factors, with socialization emerging as a prominent influencer. How individuals are socialized, their values, and the quality of their social relationships all contribute to forming a distinct happiness baseline. While stability prevails individually, the diversity in baseline happiness levels underscores the intricate interplay of intrinsic and extrinsic factors that shape the overall panorama of human contentment. Furthermore, it is essential to recognize that personality traits may only account for a fraction of the variance in happiness levels. Other influential factors, such as life circumstances, personal achievements, and health, contribute significantly to the overall happiness equation. For instance, individuals facing adversity may exhibit remarkable resilience and maintain high happiness levels, challenging the notion that personality traits determine one's happiness alone.

The preceding discussion raises the question of whether individuals can experience shifts in their happiness levels. In this context, happiness hinges on fulfilling personal desires within the realm of available options, underscoring the fundamental tenet of preference theory: getting what you want. Emotional gaps can emerge when there's a disconnect between one's desires and their realization. Emotions, as intentional states directed towards specific objects (such as feeling happy about one's life), can fluctuate due to variations in the fulfillment of desires. Some desires may carry more weight, evoking diverse emotional reactions upon fulfillment. Furthermore, happiness transcends momentary feelings to encompass broader indicators of life satisfaction, reflected in statements like "I am content with my life" or "My life is close to ideal." This intricate interplay underscores the broad nature of happiness and its subjective, context-dependent expressions.

Happiness Temporal Dimension

By acknowledging the importance of this foundational discussion, we set the stage for a comprehensive analysis that not only considers the effects of tourism on well-being but also scrutinizes the intricate interplay between individual happiness and the potential influence of tourism-related activities. This approach ensures a nuanced understanding of the subject matter, paving the way for a more informed and insightful exploration of the broader implications that tourism may have on the overall well-being of individuals.

Exploring the historical perspective of people's happiness unveils a rich tapestry of evolving beliefs and values across different epochs. In ancient times, Greek and Roman philosophers like Aristotle underscored the connection between virtuous living and personal fulfillment, laying the groundwork for early notions of eudaimonia. Religious and spiritual traditions in the East and West offered moral and spiritual guidance as pathways to happiness, intertwining the concept with notions of inner peace and moral righteousness. The Enlightenment era then ushered in a paradigm shift, emphasizing individual rights and autonomy, with thinkers like John Locke asserting happiness as a natural right. However, the Industrial Revolution redirected societal focus towards economic progress, associating happiness with material prosperity and social advancement.

Moving into the 20th century, psychological and sociological perspectives reshaped discussions on happiness. Positive psychology emerged, highlighting subjective well-being and life satisfaction. Contemporary views recognize happiness as multi-dimensional, encompassing mental health, social connections, and environmental factors. In a globalized world, cultural influences contribute diverse perspectives on a fulfilling life, challenging more universalized notions. This historical trajectory reflects the dynamic nature of human values, illustrating how societal, philosophical, and cultural shifts continuously shape perceptions and pursuits of happiness, echoing the broader evolution of human aspirations.

Essentially, the historical exploration of happiness unveils a journey from ancient philosophical ideals to contemporary, multidimensional perspectives. Each era contributes unique insights, shifting emphases on virtue, spirituality, individual rights, and economic prosperity, influencing how societies have defined and pursued happiness throughout time. Understanding this dynamic evolution provides a nuanced lens through which we can appreciate the complex interplay between historical contexts and the ever-evolving concept of human happiness.

Two Critical Questions

In our pursuit of understanding happiness through an empirical lens, we have undertaken comprehensive fieldwork across diverse countries, each with its unique context and background. Our methodology involves direct inquiries into individuals' subjective experiences by posing a fundamental question: Are you happy and satisfied with your life? The significance of these inquiries extends beyond a mere surface-level examination, as the responses obtained serve as windows into the intricate realm of emotions, personal experiences, aspirations, and inherent capabilities of the individuals under study.

The deliberate choice of posing two key questions—eliciting responses about happiness and life satisfaction—serves as a methodological cornerstone. It captured a holistic understanding of their overall well-being by directly engaging with individuals and seeking their perspectives on these integral aspects. Responses transcended mere numerical indicators or statistical data; instead, they provided profound insights into the comprehensive nature of happiness, shedding light on the nuanced interplay between subjective feelings and the broader context of one's life.

Within the broader scope of tourism literature, a prevailing assumption persists, often overlooking whether individuals at destination points are inherently happy. The standard narrative implicitly equates happiness with the perception of friendliness or characterizing a destination as a "happy island." However, a noticeable dearth of destinations explicitly acknowledge and integrate happiness as a crucial element in the co-creation of tourists' experiences. The prevailing discourse within tourism studies primarily centers around the tangible aspects of attractions, amenities, and cultural richness, neglecting the nuanced dimension of happiness as a contributing factor to the overall tourism experience.

To illustrate, consider a popular tourist destination celebrated for its picturesque landscapes and cultural diversity. While visitors may appreciate the aesthetic appeal and cultural richness, the destination's approach to understanding and fostering the inherent happiness of its residents becomes a pivotal aspect of the tourists' encounter. By incorporating happiness as a key consideration, destinations can aim for a more holistic and enriching tourist experience, fostering an environment where the local community and visitors can genuinely engage in positive, mutually beneficial interactions. Therefore, addressing the question of inherent happiness at tourist destinations not only refines our understanding of the tourist experience but also opens avenues for a more comprehensive and socially sustainable approach to tourism development.

Objectivity and Subjectivity of Happiness

Within the expansive realm of happiness literature, a pivotal distinction emerges between objective and subjective measurements of well-being. This distinction revolves around the perspective from which individuals' lives are evaluated. Objective definitions hinge upon criteria independent of an individual's subjective values and norms, grounded in an analytical theory of knowledge. However, it is crucial to acknowledge that these objective criteria, often encompassing traditional indicators such as income, consumption, socioeconomic status, and access to public services, may need to catch up in capturing the entirety of human well-being.

During my extensive fieldwork in Latin America, I often encountered scenarios where children remained home instead of attending school despite a newly constructed school being visible from their dwellings. Conversations with numerous individuals in these situations unveiled a prevalent skepticism about the future. While education was recognized as a valuable pursuit, the prospect of investing 12 years in schooling without a clear pathway to employment seemed outweighed by the immediate necessity of providing food for the family. The intricacies of human experience, emotions, and individual values must be fully encapsulated within this analytical framework, leading to a potential gap in understanding the holistic nature of well-being.

Conversely, subjective definitions of happiness center around well-being as declared by individuals. This paradigm operates on a subjective well-being/happiness approach, a prevalent perspective in relevant literature. Here, the emphasis shifts to understanding and measuring well-being from the standpoint of the individuals experiencing it. This subjective lens considers personal perceptions, emotions, and individual declarations of happiness, recognizing the inherent subjectivity that colors each person's unique experience. By adopting a subjective approach, the literature acknowledges the richness of diverse human experiences, delving into the qualitative aspects of well-being that extend beyond the confines of objective indicators.[36]

In essence, the dichotomy between objective and subjective measurements of happiness underscores the challenge of capturing the entirety of human well-being. While objective criteria provide analytical frameworks rooted in external factors, subjective perspectives explore the internal realm of personal experiences and perceptions. The nuanced exploration of these dimensions contributes to a more comprehensive understanding of human happiness's complex and multifaceted nature.

The exploration of happiness navigates a dynamic interplay between objectivity and subjectivity, forging a nuanced understanding of this intricate facet of human experience. On the objective front, conventional metrics like income, socioeconomic status, and access to public services stand as tangible measures often employed to gauge happiness. For instance, a study may correlate higher income levels with increased life satisfaction. However, the challenge arises when these objective parameters encounter the inherently subjective nature of happiness. While financial stability contributes to well-being, the emotional richness and personal fulfillment derived from relationships or meaningful experiences remain subjective and resistant to precise quantification.

Conversely, the subjective dimension of happiness invites a more personal and internal exploration of well-being. This perspective acknowledges that happiness is deeply individual, shaped by unique perspectives, values, and life circumstances. For example, an individual may report high life satisfaction due to a fulfilling career or close-knit relationships, demonstrating the subjective nature of their happiness. Yet, subjectivity introduces complexities and potential biases, making establishing universally applicable conclusions or causal relationships challenging. The

---

[36] See the Stiglitz-Sen-Fitoussi-Commission Report of 2008.

nuanced understanding of happiness emerges when researchers synergize both perspectives, recognizing the interdependence of external factors and personal experiences in shaping the overall well-being of individuals. This integrated approach allows for a richer exploration beyond mere statistics, embracing the intricate interplay of objective and subjective elements to pursue a comprehensive comprehension of human happiness.

Happiness cultivates positive individual traits such as activity, creativity, and an open mind and extends its influence on societal aspects. Happy individuals tend to excel as spouses and parents, demonstrate increased civic engagement, and exhibit informed and moderate participation in social and political spheres. Moreover, the positive effects of happiness on longevity are comparable to lifestyle factors like smoking. However, it is essential to acknowledge potential drawbacks, such as reduced risk perception and a tendency to overlook criticism. While evidence primarily addresses minor concerns, the impact of happiness on perceptions of significant matters remains an area of ongoing exploration.

Extensive research on happiness has brought to light a significant correlation, indicating that individuals who report heightened happiness levels also tend to experience a simultaneous increase in life satisfaction. For example, the correlation tends to oscillate between 0.56 and 0.50 for developed countries.[37] However, a pivotal question arises regarding the generalizability of this correlation across diverse contexts, such as small islands and developing countries. Are the observed correlation levels robustly established in the context of developed nations and similarly applicable and consistent in these distinct settings? Exploring this aspect becomes crucial to understanding the universality or potential variations in the relationship between happiness and life satisfaction across different sociocultural and economic contexts.

Driven by this compelling correlation, our analytical focus now pivots

---

[37] See Graham, C. (2009). Happiness around the world. New York: Oxford University Press.

towards unraveling the multifaceted manifestation of happiness across diverse countries. We intend to discern how happiness is perceived, encountered, and influenced amidst varied cultural, social, and economic landscapes. Through a global examination of happiness, we aspire to extract insights into the myriad factors contributing to or diminishing this emotional state. This exploration aims to provide a holistic understanding of the universal and culturally specific elements that intricately shape the pursuit of happiness globally, laying a robust foundation for the subsequent exploration of the intersection between tourism and well-being.

Happiness in Small Island Countries

Over more than a decade of dedicated research, a profound understanding of the experiences of residents in destination areas has emerged, revealing a nuanced spectrum of happiness. This phenomenon is notably conspicuous in small island destinations, as Aruba exemplifies. In this case, consistently high levels of happiness were reported, with scores reaching 78% in both 2011 and 2016 and peaking at 80.3% in 2013. The remarkable consistency of these happiness levels across different years suggests the existence of a robust and enduring pattern of contentment among residents in these tourism-centric locales. Complementary studies conducted in Curacao, Bonaire, Saba, and the Bahamas yielded analogous results, further underscoring a widespread positive sentiment among the inhabitants. Intriguingly, these scores closely align with those identified by other scholars who posit the happiness score at 76.4%.[38] This contributes to a growing body of evidence supporting enduring and notably high happiness levels in these geographical contexts.

The observation of similar happiness levels across diverse countries prompts a thought-provoking exploration into the potential universality

---

[38] See Diener, E., Lucas, R., Schimmack, U. & Helliwell, J. (2009). Wellbeing for Public Policy. New York: Oxford University Press.

of human well-being. This phenomenon suggests the existence of shared fundamental aspects of life satisfaction that transcend cultural, social, and economic disparities. Possible explanations include universal human needs and aspirations, such as a desire for purpose, social connections, economic stability, and personal fulfillment. Globalization and the dissemination of information and cultural influences across borders also contribute to the convergence of happiness levels as individuals adopt similar lifestyles and aspirations.

However, it is crucial to approach such observations with an awareness of the unique cultural, historical, and contextual factors that shape individual experiences within each country. Recognizing both the commonalities and diversities in the pursuit of happiness can offer valuable insights for policymakers, researchers, and individuals seeking to enhance overall well-being on a global scale.

Consider the case of the Bahamas, where my colleagues at the University of the West Indies and I researched the highly developed tourist island of New Providence in 2018. Respondents revealed an impressive overall happiness score of 81.2%. To delve deeper into this happiness score, we posed additional questions, such as "In most ways, my life is close to being ideal" and "The conditions of my life are excellent." The former assesses aspirations, while the latter measures capabilities. Strikingly, scores for aspirations closely aligned with the ideal, registering a mean of 3.31, and capabilities yielded a mean score of 3.27.

Notably, no statistically significant differences were identified between the two. This congruence in scores indicates that individuals in the Bahamas, on average, find themselves in a state where their aspirations closely mirror their perceived capabilities. The absence of statistical significance in the capabilities dimension further reinforces that individuals are not experiencing a shortfall in realizing their goals compared to their perceived capacities. This insight sheds light on a positive alignment between aspirations and capabilities, suggesting that individuals in the

Bahamas are, on average, achieving what they set out to accomplish in various aspects of their lives.

Nevertheless, it is intriguing to observe that both the aspiration and capability scores fall below the respondents' overall happiness rating of 4.06, prompting a deeper investigation into the complex interplay among aspirations, capabilities, and the subjective experience of happiness in this particular context. The revelation that both aspiration and capability scores lag behind the overarching happiness metric adds a layer to the discourse. This suggests that, despite the acknowledged disparity between individual aspirations and actual capabilities, individuals in the Bahamas, on average, still express a notably high level of overall happiness. This phenomenon implies that factors beyond the strict alignment of aspirations and capabilities play a substantial role in shaping happiness, potentially encompassing elements such as robust social connections, cultural influences, or individual resilience. Respondents appear to adapt to the realistic opportunities available, as reflected in the reported mean score of 3.42 on the question "I am satisfied with my life."

The intriguing disparity between a lower score on satisfaction with life (3.42) and a higher score on overall happiness (4.06) in the Bahamas prompts a nuanced exploration of subjective well-being. The correlation between happiness and satisfaction with life is .383 (p=0.000). The correlation coefficient of .383 between happiness and satisfaction with life suggests a moderate positive relationship between the two variables. This indicates that as one's happiness increases, there tends to be a corresponding increase in satisfaction with life and vice versa. The p-value of 0.000 indicates that this correlation is statistically significant, suggesting that it is unlikely to have occurred by random chance alone.

While a positive correlation exists between happiness and satisfaction with life, it does not necessarily mean that one directly causes the other. Other factors, such as individual personality traits, life circumstances, cultural influences, and societal norms, could also play significant roles in shaping happiness and satisfaction with life. The strength of the correlation, while moderate, indicates that while happiness and satisfaction with life are related, they are not entirely synonymous. One can experience moments of happiness without overall satisfaction with life and vice versa.

While the elevated happiness score signifies a strong positive evaluation of immediate emotional experiences, the slightly lower satisfaction with life score suggests a more comprehensive assessment of broader life domains. This distinction may indicate that, despite high positive emotions, individuals harbor concerns or dissatisfaction in specific aspects of their lives. Cultural and societal expectations may contribute to this gap, as individuals may gauge happiness based on immediate emotional states. In contrast, unmet aspirations or perceived societal benchmarks could influence satisfaction with life.

Moreover, the adaptability of respondents to their realistic opportunities and challenges becomes evident, as the lower satisfaction with life score may reflect an acknowledgment of areas for improvement while still deriving a high level of happiness from navigating and appreciating positive aspects of life. In this context, the lower satisfaction with life score despite a higher level of happiness suggests that individuals are resilient in acknowledging areas of their lives that require improvement. Rather than being overwhelmed or disheartened by these challenges, they demonstrate resilience by recognizing areas for growth and adaptation. This acknowledgment of areas for improvement reflects an ability to confront and address obstacles, an essential aspect of resilience.

Furthermore, individuals can still derive happiness from navigating and appreciating positive aspects of life despite lower satisfaction, with life scores underscoring their resilience. Despite facing difficulties or unmet aspirations, they can find joy and fulfillment. This ability to maintain a positive outlook and experience happiness in adversity exemplifies resilience.

This multifaceted perspective underscores the importance of considering various dimensions of well-being to comprehensively understand and effectively enhance individuals' overall life satisfaction.

Notably, it is crucial to acknowledge that all these studies were conducted before the onset of the COVID-19 pandemic.

Happiness and Comparing to Each Other

The intriguing aspect of happiness dynamics among island residents becomes even more pronounced when examining the phenomenon of residents feeling less happy when making comparisons with others. This psychological nuance sheds light on the complex interplay between individual happiness perceptions and societal benchmarks, uncovering insights that contribute to a more comprehensive understanding of well-being in these island destinations. The tendency for respondents to perceive lower happiness levels when comparing themselves to others unveils a social dimension influencing individual contentment. This phenomenon aligns with social comparison theory, a psychological concept suggesting that individuals determine their social and personal worth based on how they stack up against others.

By 2015, my colleagues and I at the University of Central Florida Rosen College researched the island of Aruba, inquiring into residents' happiness. As indicated earlier, Aruba residents showed a remarkable consistency in their happiness level, with a mean score oscillating between 76% and 80%. The research identified four distinct resident groups clustered by generation, income, education level, place of work, time judgment (past, present, and future), and happiness. The study named the groups as follows: *Vintage Tourism Believers*, *Noble Ambassadors of Happiness*, *Optimistic Happy Tourism Successors*, and *Optimistic Happy Tourism Amigos*. In the table below, one can see the apparent differences between the groups regarding *Happiness* and *Comparison of Life Situation* between the groups.

Examining social comparison about happiness yielded compelling and consistent findings, revealing a robust and significant positive association (β=0.40; p<0.000). This result echoes the observations made in 2011[39], reinforcing the enduring impact of social comparison on individuals' subjective well-being. In the context of Aruba, respondents indicated that social comparison, particularly prevalent as an upward comparison, involves measuring oneself against those perceived to possess superior abilities and attributes.

Examining the relationship between social comparison and equality reveals a nuanced interplay within the context of Aruba. The positive association between social comparison and happiness suggests that Aruba predominantly engages in upward social comparison, where they measure themselves against those perceived to possess superior attributes. This inclination towards favorable social comparison aligns with the societal changes indicated by a reduced Gini coefficient[40] from 0.4 to 0.37, signifying a movement towards greater equality.[41] The evolving sociological landscape of Aruba, marked by a diminishing wealth gap, may contribute to a climate where individuals feel empowered to engage in social comparison without experiencing significant negative emotional impacts. The positive relationship observed underscores the potential benefits of societal movements toward greater equality in individual well-being, emphasizing the significance of social and economic fairness.

However, it is crucial to recognize that the dynamics between social

---

[39] See Croes, R. et al. (2011). *Winning the future. Tourism master plan.* Dick Pope Sr. Institute *for* Tourism Studies, September.

[40] The Gini coefficient is a measure of economic inequality within a population. It is typically used to assess income or wealth distribution. The coefficient is between 0 and 1, where 0 represents perfect equality (everyone has the same income or wealth), and 1 signifies perfect inequality (one person or household has all the income or wealth). In simple terms, a higher Gini coefficient indicates greater economic inequality.

[41] Croes, R., Rivera, M and Semrad, K. (2017). *Aruba happiness and tourism.* Dick Pope Sr. Institute *for* Tourism Studies, September.

comparison and equality are complex and can be influenced by various factors. Social comparison may lead to contrasting emotions in societies marked by pronounced inequality, including inadequacy or envy. Thus, efforts to address social and economic disparities contribute to societal fairness and foster a healthier social comparison dynamic. Understanding these nuanced interactions is essential for policymakers aiming to create conditions that promote equality and contribute positively to the overall psychological well-being of individuals within a society.

Table 1. Respondents' Perceptions by Cluster

	Vintage Tourism Believers	Noble Ambassadors of Happiness	Optimistic Happy Tourism Successors	Optimistic Happy Tourism Amigos
Comparison of Life Situation				
Worse than others	19.2%	16.2%		
Same as others	32.7%	66.2%		
Better than others	48.1%	17.5%	100.0%	100.0%
Optimism	3.13	3.11	3.32	3.38
	(a)	(a)	(b)	(b)
Happiness	3.63	3.49	4.25	4.33
	(a)	(a)	(b)	(b)

Note: Note: (a) significantly lower than (b). Adopted from Croes, R., Rivera, M and Semrad, K. (2017). *Aruba happiness and tourism*. Dick Pope Sr. Institute for Tourism Studies, September.

In the context of island communities, where social bonds and connections are often intense, the impact of these social comparisons on happiness becomes particularly intriguing. Take, for instance, a scenario in a small Caribbean Island where residents share close relationships within a tightly woven community fabric. In such an environment, individuals may inadvertently engage in social comparisons with their neighbors, friends, and family members. The flourishing social connections could lead to heightened awareness of others' achievements, lifestyles, or perceived happiness, creating a subtle yet impactful backdrop for individual self-evaluations.

Or, consider a situation where one island resident, inspired by a peer's success or apparent contentment, starts to reassess their own life satisfaction. The comparative nature of social interactions within the community might induce a sense of competition or a desire to conform to certain societal norms. This dynamic can be intensified in smaller island settings, where individuals may share common cultural backgrounds and histories, making social comparisons more immediate and influential.

In another illustration, residents participating in communal events, such as local festivals or gatherings, may experience a heightened awareness of their standing within the social hierarchy. The joyous celebrations and shared moments of success during these events may prompt individuals to gauge their happiness levels relative to the perceived happiness of their peers. The proximity and interconnectedness in island communities can amplify the impact of such social comparisons, influencing individual perceptions of contentment and fulfillment.

Furthermore, the prevalence of social media in island communities adds a modern twist to these dynamics. Residents, interconnected through digital platforms, may be exposed to curated representations of others' lives, contributing to a constant stream of social comparisons. For instance, seeing peers' travel experiences, material possessions, or professional achievements online might lead individuals to reassess their happiness levels, potentially fostering a sense of inadequacy or unfulfillment.

Happiness and Generational Differences

Examining the generational differences in this pattern adds a layer of complexity. These generational differences in happiness within a small island context carry significant implications for understanding the evolving dynamics of well-being and satisfaction across different age groups. These distinctions not only reflect varying life experiences and societal influences but also provide valuable insights into the broader cultural and environmental factors shaping happiness within the unique social fabric of island communities.

To illustrate, exploring happiness distribution within an island unveils notable variances. In 2017 Curacao, the analysis reveals significant disparities in happiness levels across different generations. Generation Z exhibits the lowest happiness score at 64.8%, in stark contrast to markedly higher scores observed for Boomers (78.7%), Generation X (79.5%), and Generation Y (79.7%). When residents assess their happiness relative to others, the overall mean score is 72.2%, indicating that seven out of ten respondents perceive themselves as happier than their peers and friends. Nevertheless, there are variations in scores among generations, with Generation Z once again reporting the lowest score (69.3%), followed by Boomers (70.2%), Generation X (71.5%), and Generation Y (75.4%).

Interestingly, respondents tend to feel less happy than others, revealing a nuanced aspect of happiness dynamics among island residents. It is important to note that contextual conditions may influence generational differences. Unlike Curacao, Aruba does not exhibit a similar pattern, as there are no discernible differences across generations.

The observed differences in happiness distribution between Aruba and Curacao prompt exploring the potential contextual factors shaping subjective well-being on each island. In Curacao, significant variations across generations indicate that age-related perspectives contribute to distinct happiness levels. The generational discrepancy, particularly in social comparison dynamics, highlights the intricate interplay of societal influences on individual perceptions of happiness. The tendency of survey participants to experience reduced happiness when comparing themselves to others adds an extra level of difficulty to the overall happiness scenario in Curacao. On the other hand, Aruba presents a contrasting pattern, with no apparent generational differences in happiness levels. This suggests that unique contextual conditions and societal factors on the island contribute to a more consistent experience of happiness across different age groups. Analyzing potential drivers such as economic stability, social structures, and cultural influences is essential for comprehending the nuanced variations in happiness outcomes between the two Caribbean islands.

The potential discrepancy in happiness results underscores the need to consider the diverse socio-economic and cultural contexts that shape subjective well-being. Economic conditions, access to opportunities, and the overall sociocultural climate may play pivotal roles in influencing how individuals perceive happiness within a given society. Moreover, policy initiatives, community engagement, and the availability of social support may contribute to the observed variations. Understanding these nuanced factors is crucial for policymakers aiming to enhance the overall quality of life for residents in Aruba and Curacao. By recognizing and addressing the unique societal dynamics at play, interventions can be tailored to meet the specific well-being needs of each island, fostering a more comprehensive and practical approach to promoting happiness and life satisfaction.

Happiness in Developing Economies

During our extensive research conducted between 2012 and 2014 in Mexico, Costa Rica, and Ecuador, my colleague Manuel Rivera and I delved into the intricate realm of subjective well-being.[42] Our central inquiry, encapsulated in the question, "In general, I consider myself a happy person," revealed a striking and consistent trend. Respondents from these Latin American countries consistently reported elevated happiness levels, ranging from 74.4% in Mexico to 78.6% in Costa Rica and 74.6% in Ecuador. Surprisingly, these figures closely paralleled the high happiness indices observed in developed nations such as Finland, Scandinavian countries, and small island countries.

The intriguing aspect of our findings lies in the paradoxical relationship

---

[42] Croes, R. & Rivera, M. (2016). *Poverty Alleviation through Tourism Development: A Comprehensive and Integrated Approach.* Apple Academic Press: Waretown, NJ, USA.

between reported happiness and the prevalent challenges of poverty and inequality within the Latin American context. Despite facing higher levels of economic disparity and lower socioeconomic indicators than their Scandinavian counterparts, individuals in Mexico, Costa Rica, and Ecuador expressed comparable or even higher happiness levels. This raises compelling questions about the interplay between material conditions and subjective well-being.

One possible lens through which to interpret these findings is the role of social and cultural factors in shaping perceptions of happiness. Tight-knit communities, strong social connections, and cultural resilience in Latin American societies may contribute to communal well-being that transcends economic challenges. Additionally, cultural emphasis on familial ties and community support structures could serve as buffers against the adverse effects of poverty. However, it is crucial to acknowledge that this apparent paradox still needs to diminish the significance of addressing poverty and inequality. While happiness reports suggest a remarkable resilience in the face of adversity, persistent economic disparities undoubtedly impact various aspects of individuals' lives, including access to education, healthcare, and overall quality of life. As we delve deeper into understanding the dynamics of happiness amidst economic challenges, it becomes imperative to consider the reported subjective well-being and the tangible impacts of poverty and inequality on the overall welfare of individuals and communities.

A noteworthy distinction emerged when examining the happiness levels of respondents across the three countries in our study. Costa Rican respondents stood out significantly, reporting higher happiness levels than their counterparts in Ecuador and Mexico. Interestingly, Ecuador and Mexico displayed almost identical values in terms of happiness, indicating a striking similarity in the reported subjective well-being of individuals in these two nations. Delving deeper into the nuances of individual perceptions, an intriguing pattern surfaced in Mexico. Respondents in Mexico expressed relatively higher happiness levels when comparing themselves to their peers, in contrast to their self-assessment as happy individuals. This phenomenon contrasts the patterns observed in Ecuador and Costa Rica, where respondents seemed to align their self-perception of happiness more closely with their assessment in a broader context.

This discrepancy suggests variations in how individuals in Mexico, Ecuador, and Costa Rica interpret and express their happiness. The cultural and social frameworks within these countries may play a pivotal role in shaping the subjective experience of happiness. Understanding these distinctions not only enriches our comprehension of cultural differences in the perception of happiness but also underscores the importance of considering diverse cultural lenses when assessing well-being. Further exploring the cultural dynamics that influence these perceptions can provide valuable insights into the complex interplay between individual attitudes, societal values, and the subjective experience of happiness in different regions.

Significant disparities in happiness become apparent when examining various income brackets. We categorized the population into five groups, each comprising twenty percent, referred to as quintiles. Quintiles are a statistical tool widely employed in analyzing numerical data like income or test scores to grasp distribution patterns within a population. In our study, quintiles one and two consistently report lower perceived happiness than their counterparts in quintiles four and five. Interestingly, those in quintiles four and five consistently rate their happiness higher than individuals in other quintiles. This nuanced exploration sheds light on the intricate relationship between economic status and subjective well-being. Moreover, our analysis extends beyond economic factors, revealing that age and life course also influence happiness, with discernible patterns among individuals in Generation Y and Boomers.

Despite the universal human tendency to evaluate subjective well-being, diverse factors contribute to shaping these assessments. Individuals navigate their assessments based on a complex interplay of past experiences, future expectations, and comparative evaluations with others. Our findings challenge the notion that all individuals assess their subjective well-being in the same way, as variations across income groups and age cohorts underscore the nuanced nature of these evaluations.

The impact of context and circumstances on subjective well-being further complicates the understanding of happiness. Our observations align with existing literature, emphasizing that external factors, including social, cultural, and economic contexts, are crucial in shaping individual perceptions of happiness. This multidimensional perspective reinforces the need for a comprehensive approach to studying subjective well-being, acknowledging the intricate interplay between personal experiences, societal influences, and the broader contextual backdrop. As we delve deeper into the intricacies of happiness assessment, acknowledging these multifaceted influences becomes essential for a holistic understanding of the diverse elements that contribute to the subjective experience of well-being.

Happiness and the Poor

In our analysis of Colombia, my coauthors and I focused on the impoverished population, a departure from previous studies.[43] Our fieldwork took us to La Candelaria in Bogota and La Macarena in Meta. Notably, the only existing study conducted in Colombia, the Happiness Diagnosis in 2015, revealed intriguing insights. According to this study, 88.6% of individuals express satisfaction with their lives, while 83% report feeling happy. Furthermore, 57.3% experience low preoccupation and 76.4% do not feel depressed.

Digging deeper into the data, a nuanced picture emerges. Younger individuals exhibit higher satisfaction and happiness levels than their older counterparts, suggesting a generational divide. Additionally, there

---

[43] Croes, R., Rivera, M., Bonilla, J. & Ridderstaat, J. (2019). Tourism, income and experienced poverty. 7th Conference IATE, La Plata, Argentina, September 1-2.

is a stark contrast between those who perceive themselves as poor and others, with the former being significantly less satisfied and happy. A similar pattern is observed when comparing individuals with sufficient income to meet their needs versus those who struggle financially.

A notable disparity is evident when examining rural versus urban settings. Residents in rural areas tend to report lower levels of happiness and satisfaction, coupled with higher rates of preoccupation and depression. This rural-urban divide in Colombia highlights a substantial poverty gap that demands attention and necessitates exploring potential solutions.

One avenue of interest is the role of tourism development in addressing these disparities. We expect tourism to play a pivotal role in transforming the dire situation, fostering human development, and enhancing overall happiness. To delve deeper into this hypothesis, we undertake a comparative analysis of two distinct territories within Colombia.

The first territory is in Bogota, the capital city, serving as a traditional tourism destination. The second territory is La Macarena in Meta, a post-conflict region in the south characterized by a tumultuous past and a prolonged lack of opportunities. However, it has undergone a remarkable transformation through tourism development. By juxtaposing these two territories, we aim to gain insights into the potential impact of tourism on human development and happiness, particularly in regions grappling with historical challenges.

Based on the 2017 data, Colombia grapples with significant poverty challenges, with 26.9% of the population falling below the poverty line and 7.4% below the extreme poverty line. The national Gini coefficient stands at 0.508, indicating substantial income inequality. In Bogota, the capital city, 12.4% of the population resides below the poverty line, 2.4% below the extreme poverty line, with a Gini coefficient of 0.499. In Meta, the region housing La Macarena, 25.1% experience monetary poverty, 7.6% endure extreme monetary poverty, and the Gini coefficient is 0.473.

Adopting the capability approach, the Multidimensional Poverty Index expands the understanding of poverty by incorporating various dimensions. These include educational conditions at home, childhood and youth, work, health, and access to public services and dwelling conditions. According to this index, 17% of the Colombian population lives in poverty, with rural areas bearing the brunt at 36.6%. In contrast, Bogota exhibits a lower incidence of multidimensional poverty at 5.9%, while the Central Region reports 18% of the population experiencing poverty.

Another crucial metric is the quality-of-life survey based on The Living Standards Measurement Study by the World Bank, which aims for evidence-based policymaking. This measurement focuses on objective aspects and dimensions of household well-being. Health and education emerge as particularly unequal variables in the quality-of-life approach. The urban-rural divide is stark, with 58.6% of urban households having internet access compared to a mere 17% in rural areas, underscoring the substantial inequality in these fundamental aspects of life. This disparity calls for targeted policy interventions to address the wide-ranging challenges different regions in Colombia face.

In our research, we gauged the happiness of impoverished individuals by posing, "I like to enjoy life no matter what and make the most of everything." The mean happiness score stood at 3.590, with a standard deviation of 1.105. This signifies that, on average, 71.8% of respondents expressed happiness. Participants were further asked to rank ten life domains in terms of their significance to their happiness: money, friends, education, health, food, family, recreation, violence, and recognition. Employing a Mann-Whitney U analysis, our results revealed that health, education, family, food, and work emerged as the most pivotal life domains for those in poverty. The ranking order suggests a prioritization of physical functioning, followed closely by social functioning, highlighting the values held by the impoverished. These findings align with our earlier research in Latin American countries, specifically Mexico, Costa Rica, and Ecuador.

While the ranking order of life domains appears similar for impoverished individuals residing in urban and rural areas, notable differences arise in social functioning. Specifically, a statistically significant disparity is observed in the family and friends' domains, with the mean score in the urban area surpassing that in the rural area ($p<0.01$). Intriguingly, despite the acknowledged importance of money, it occupies a lower rank than the preceding two functionings.

Furthermore, the results reveal a noteworthy incongruity between income poverty (31%) and experienced poverty (10%). Participants were asked to rate their agreement with "I am satisfied with my life," with 81% expressing high satisfaction levels. A subsequent t-test examined whether there was a statistically significant difference in mean life satisfaction between urban (La Candelaria) and rural (La Macarena) areas. Strikingly, individuals in the rural area exhibited higher life satisfaction compared to their urban counterparts ($p<0.01$). Additionally, the study explored the relationship between average life satisfaction and its standard deviation, treating well-being as a continuous variable. The findings indicate a high average life satisfaction (81%) coupled with a low standard deviation of life satisfaction (SD= 0.90), akin to patterns observed in developed countries.

The correlation analysis reveals no statistically significant relationship between income and the experience of poverty. Surprisingly, fewer than 10% of the individuals categorized as poor reported experiencing poverty. This discrepancy becomes evident when comparing the percentage of income-poor individuals (31%) with those who self-report experiencing poverty (10%). Moreover, the study indicates that despite economic challenges, a substantial majority of the poor (81%) express high satisfaction with their overall life. Interestingly, when comparing rural (La Macarena) and urban (La Candelaria) areas, the results suggest that individuals in the rural setting exhibit greater life satisfaction than their urban counterparts. The satisfaction difference is statistically significant, with a p-value less than 0.01. This sheds light on the nuanced relationship between geographical location and life satisfaction among the economically disadvantaged.

The analysis also reveals a significant positive correlation between life satisfaction and aspirations (p < 0.01). Respondents from La Candelaria, on average, report higher levels of life aspirations (M=3.34; SD=1.44) compared to those from La Macarena (M=3.01; SD=1.26), and this difference is statistically significant with a p-value less than 0.05. These results highlight the intricate interplay between subjective well-being, geographic location, and economic circumstances among the impoverished population.

We delved into the respondents' choices and capabilities in two distinct regions of Colombia by exploring their agreement with two statements: "In many aspects, my life is close to ideal" (reflecting aspirations) and "My life conditions are excellent" (indicating achieved capabilities). The mean score for the first statement in La Candelaria was 3.51 out of 5 (SD=1.00), while in La Macarena, it was M=3.33, SD=1.01, and these mean scores did not exhibit statistical differences. Similarly, concerning capabilities, the mean score for La Candelaria was 3.38 (SD=1.01), and for La Macarena, it was 3.30 with SD=1.02, again showing no statistically significant differences.

This lack of statistical distinction between the two regions suggests the respondents' lack of an aspiration gap or unfulfilled capabilities. Interestingly, the mean scores for aspirations and capabilities were lower than the mean for overall life satisfaction, which was 4.14. This implies that while individuals in both regions may not perceive their lives as ideal or excellent in all aspects, they report relatively high overall life satisfaction. These findings underscore the complexity of individuals' perceptions and priorities, suggesting that aspirations and capabilities, while distinct, do not significantly differ across the studied regions. It prompts further exploration into the factors contributing to the overall life satisfaction reported by respondents despite variations in specific aspects of their lives.

In our investigation, we sought to understand the relationship between happiness and satisfaction with life. The correlation analysis revealed intriguing insights: in La Macarena, the correlation coefficient stands at 0.4206 (p < .05), while in La Candelaria, it is slightly lower at 0.2166 (p

< .05). These moderate correlation scores unveil a nuanced picture. They suggest a significant association between happiness and life satisfaction yet hint at their distinctiveness. While happiness and satisfaction with life often go hand in hand, they are not entirely interchangeable. It is possible to experience fleeting moments of joy without overall life satisfaction, and conversely, one might find contentment despite occasional bouts of unhappiness. This duality underscores the complexity of human emotions and the multifaceted nature of what it means to lead a fulfilling life.

Happiness in a Small Tourism City

Our examination of well-being extended to the charming small city of Sopot in Poland, which is characterized as an urban area with a population of fewer than 100,000 people. Nestled along the Baltic coast, Sopot provides a distinctive context for our assessment, offering a unique blend of urban living within the parameters of a smaller community setting. Exploring well-being in Sopot contributes valuable insights into the dynamics of smaller urban environments, shedding light on the factors influencing the quality of life in such locales. Sopot is a picturesque city on the Baltic Sea coast in northern Poland. As one of the country's well-known resort towns, Sopot holds a special place with its natural beauty, historic charm, and modern amenities. Renowned for its sandy beaches, Sopot is a popular destination for locals and tourists seeking a seaside retreat.

The city is characterized by its unique architecture, blending traditional elements with contemporary design. One of the notable landmarks is the iconic wooden pier, extending gracefully into the Baltic Sea and offering panoramic views of the coastline. The lively atmosphere along the dock and its cafes, restaurants, and entertainment options add to the city's vibrant character. Sopot is a coastal gem and a cultural hub featuring various events and festivals throughout the year. The city's cultural scene includes theaters, art galleries, and music venues, contributing to its reputation as a dynamic and lively destination.

In the summer of 2018, a collaborative effort between researchers from the University of Gdansk and our UCF Rosen College team led to data collection in Sopot, employing convenience sampling on a first-come, first-serve basis. To address potential sampling bias, quota sampling based on demographic criteria such as age, gender, and occupation was utilized. This approach ensured that the survey results would accurately represent the diverse population of Sopot. The sampled individuals' demographics, including age, gender, marital status, education, income, and district representation, closely mirrored the distribution of the broader Sopot population, enhancing the overall reliability and representativeness of the findings.

Upon analyzing the survey results, 85.2% of participants self-identified as experiencing happiness, aligning with established happiness research, suggesting a typical happiness score ranging from 70% to 80%. However, a nuanced perspective emerged when exploring life satisfaction, with a comparatively lower 74.2% expressing contentment. The mean satisfaction score of 3.71 and a standard deviation of 1.129 revealed a noteworthy gap between individual optimism and societal pessimism. This discrepancy suggests that individuals in Sopot perceive a degree of control over their happiness, even in the face of broader societal challenges. It indicates that while respondents acknowledge certain limitations in achieving their life aspirations, they maintain a positive outlook on their immediate experiences.

Remarkably, respondents from Sopot exhibited a higher degree of pessimism about the future, consistent with earlier investigations. This underscores the intricate interplay between individual happiness and broader societal perspectives within the specific context of Sopot. An intriguing aspect is that the average happiness score surpassed the satisfaction-with-life score, highlighting the multifaceted nature of happiness encompassing experiential-emotional and evaluative-cognitive dimensions. Despite expressing lower satisfaction with their overall lives, respondents in Sopot seem to derive contentment from day-to-day experiences, indicating a nuanced understanding of happiness beyond fulfilling long-term aspirations.

The noticeable contrast between life satisfaction and happiness scores presents compelling insights into the depopulation trend observed in Sopot, as outlined in the Sopot Development Strategy for 2022-2030. In our investigation,[44] the correlation between happiness and satisfaction with life registers at 0.333, with a significance level of $p<0.001$. This discovery echoes the situation in the Bahamas, where the correlation is moderate. The moderate correlation indicates that while happiness and life satisfaction are related, they are not entirely interchangeable. This complexity suggests that individuals in Sopot may experience happiness from various sources beyond overall life satisfaction, such as immediate emotional experiences or specific aspects of their lives.

Understanding this complexity is crucial for developing strategies that cater to the community's diverse needs and aspirations, addressing the unique challenges presented by the interplay of individual perceptions and societal trends in this specific urban context.

Lessons Learned

The innate human desire to experience positive emotions while avoiding negative ones underscores the intrinsic value placed on feeling good. Happiness, as a sought-after state, holds significance not only as an inherent good but also for its potential to contribute to the success and effective functioning of a society. However, an essential consideration arises when individuals maintain constant happiness regardless of their living conditions. In such instances, there is a risk of complacency among societal leaders who may need more motivation to instigate necessary changes for improving overall well-being.

The critical question then emerges: Can happiness be actively improved?

---

[44] Croes, R., Shapoval, V., Rivera, M., Bak, M. & Zientara, P. (2024). Promoting Residents' Happiness Through a Human-Centric Approach to Tourism City Development. *International Journal of Tourism Cities*, https://doi.org/10.1108/ IJTC-05-2023-0105.

Ample research indicates that happiness is not static; it can evolve, and interventions have the potential to make a meaningful difference in people's lives. This remains true despite individual differences in personality, aspirations, motivations, and external life conditions.In the subsequent chapter, a comprehensive exploration of the determinants of happiness will be undertaken to elucidate further the arresting factors influencing the pursuit and attainment of well-being.

Tourism and the
Determinants of Well-being

In the preceding chapter, I assumed a connection exists between tourism development and well-being. In the current chapter, I aim to scrutinize and validate this assumption by exploring my research across various countries. Beyond merely confirming this link, I will look into the gripping drivers that contribute to shaping this relationship if any discernible factors emerge.

Embarking on this investigative journey, I will look for empirical evidence to prove the presumed correlation between tourism development and well-being and analyze the underlying forces at play. By dissecting the multifaceted aspects of this relationship, I will unravel the complexities and identify the key elements that act as drivers, potentially influencing the symbiotic interplay between tourism development and the overall well-being of individuals and communities. As I delve into diverse case studies and empirical data, the objective is to understand the dynamics governing this connection comprehensively. This analytical exploration will go beyond a mere acknowledgment of the existence of a relationship, aiming to uncover the intricacies of the link and shed light on the contextual nuances that shape the interdependence between tourism development and well-being.

To thoroughly analyze the connection between tourism and well-being, it is crucial to consider three key dimensions: relevance, orientation, and extent, each bearing implications for residents. Relevance underscores the importance of this correlation, given that tourism profoundly affects the well-being of individuals and communities. For instance, well-being can be viewed as a strategic asset, presenting opportunities for bolstering tourism arrivals and cultivating a more vibrant visitor economy. Orientation delves into the directionality of the impact, shedding light on whether the relationship is positive, negative, or neutral for residents. For instance, analyzing the orientation of mass tourism in a residential area can reveal the potential drawbacks of increased congestion, noise, and strain on local resources, negatively impacting residents' overall well-being. Extent examines the scale of tourism's impact and how the four tourism development dimensions impact residents.

The Empirical Nexus

Before examining the factors influencing the dynamic interplay between tourism and well-being, it is crucial to establish the existence of this connection. This initial investigation seeks to determine whether tourism acts as a catalyst for well-being or if well-being stimulates tourism. Additionally, the nature of this relationship must be discerned, questioning whether it follows a linear cause-and-effect pattern or is characterized by a more complex and non-linear dynamic. The primary goal of this inquiry is to unveil the presence of a reciprocal dynamic between tourism and well-being, exploring whether engagement in tourism activities positively contributes to individuals' overall well-being or if the existing state of well-being propels individuals to partake in tourism endeavors. Unraveling these fundamental questions validates the assumed link between tourism and well-being and fosters a more nuanced understanding of the underlying dynamics.

In exploring this relationship, focusing on islands in the Caribbean and the Mediterranean, Central and South America, Eastern Europe, and

Asia, we scrutinize the connection between tourism and well-being using objective and subjective criteria. Employing various econometric techniques, this analysis spans regions such as Aruba, the Bahamas, Malta, Poland, seven Central American countries, ten South American countries, and Malaysia. The research delves into objective and subjective examination of the relationship, covering the same countries and others while employing different statistical techniques. The progression of tourism not only bolsters societal material resources but also individualizes available resources, enhancing incomes, skills, and information. This, in turn, nurtures the augmentation of physical and intellectual capacities among people, supporting overall well-being by broadening choices and opportunities, thereby contributing to a healthier and more fulfilling life.

Tourists, drawn to distinctive experiences, deem interaction with residents pivotal in shaping and enriching their travel encounters. The proficiency and insights of residents thus play a crucial role in crafting satisfying tourist experiences. This satisfaction, in turn, can fuel increased expenditure, bolstering the destination's resources and fostering a more sustainable and resilient community. Moreover, the link between tourism development and well-being transcends mere economic gains, as evidenced by the preference of international tourists for countries with higher happiness indices.

The impact on well-being manifests through direct and indirect channels, with economic expansion as a primary conduit. This intricate interplay is influenced by various factors such as productivity, coordination, resource allocation, and demand elasticity. Enhanced community well-being can catalyze tourism growth, underscoring the nuanced dynamics shaping the strength and nature of these interconnections. Thus, a comprehensive understanding of these dynamics provides insight into the symbiotic relationship between tourism and well-being, revealing its multifaceted outcomes.

This understanding underscores the compelling nature of tourism development, which spans economic, social, cultural, and environmental dimensions. It highlights the significance of cultural and socio-economic factors in shaping perceptions of happiness. Thus, a holistic understanding of the relationship between tourism development and subjective well-being necessitates considering many factors.

Empirical Manifestations

In 2019, I and two colleagues at Rosen College conducted a comprehensive study covering ten South American countries that provided insights into the region's tourism industry, indicating the need for further development initiatives given economic growth disparities and persistent poverty rates.[45] The analysis of the period from 1998 to 2014 revealed a dynamic and interdependent relationship between tourism development and well-being measured by the human development index (HDI), challenging traditional linear models. The study highlighted threshold effects, exemplified by Venezuela's regression, suggesting that shifts in one dimension can lead to abrupt changes in the other. Context-specific analyses emphasized the non-universal uniformity of this connection across regions and nations. However, the study's limitations were acknowledged — particularly its reliance on macroeconomic indicators — neglecting in-country lifestyle differences and a full spectrum of factors affecting human development.

The study emphasized the unidirectional relationship between tourism development and well-being, with the relationship running from the latter to tourism development. While the study highlighted the importance of rising incomes from tourism for human development, it cautioned against assuming a direct translation of income growth into human development performance. The distribution of tourism benefits and the allocation of receipts to support public health, education, safety, and other human development were deemed critical considerations.

---

[45] See Croes, R., Ridderstaat, J. & Shapoval, V. (2020). Extending tourism competitiveness to human development. Annals of Tourism Research, 80, January (102825).

In examining various cases, the relationship between tourism development and well-being emerges as a dynamic and multifaceted phenomenon. Malta's experience illustrates a clear and positive association between tourism growth and well-being, with notable short-term benefits and promising long-term prospects. Similarly, Aruba's case underscores a reciprocal relationship between tourism development and well-being, validated objectively through metrics like the Human Development Index (HDI), and subjectively through feedback from a substantial sample size of 450 participants. This dual confirmation highlights the comprehensive impact of tourism on overall societal welfare.

Colombia's thorough investigation into the relationship between tourism and well-being sheds light on the profound potential of tourism to uplift living standards, especially among economically disadvantaged individuals residing in urban and rural locales. This study underscores tourism's critical role in fostering socioeconomic advancement and addressing inequalities across diverse geographic settings by explicitly targeting marginalized populations. The findings from Colombia's examination highlight how tourism initiatives can serve as catalysts for positive change, offering opportunities for income generation, employment, and community development in regions where such opportunities are scarce. Moreover, by focusing on urban and rural areas, the study provides a comprehensive understanding of how tourism can impact different segments of society, regardless of their geographical location.

Conversely, studies conducted in Costa Rica and Nicaragua suggest a more nuanced relationship characterized by threshold effects. While tourism contributes to well-being, its effects may vary depending on specific thresholds, particularly emphasizing its vital role in bolstering well-being at lower developmental levels. Furthermore, a panel study encompassing Central American countries and Malaysia illuminates a bidirectional relationship between tourism development and well-being. Bidirectionality denotes a reciprocal influence, wherein tourism enhances well-being and derives momentum from improved societal well-being. This finding underscores the complex interplay between tourism growth and societal welfare, indicating that each influences and reinforces the other in a continuous feedback loop.

The comprehensive study of the intricate relationship between tourism development and well-being provides nuanced insights into the complex interplay of these variables. It encompasses diverse regions like Poland, South American countries, Ecuador, and Malaysia and specific cases such as Malta and Aruba. Recognizing the multidimensional nature of tourism development, the study underscores the pivotal role of cultural and socio-economic factors in shaping happiness perceptions. While results vary across regions, common themes emerge, including the dynamic and interdependent relationship challenging traditional models, the significance of context-specific analyses, and the necessity for careful distribution of tourism benefits. The findings emphasize the need for nuanced exploration incorporating macroeconomic indicators and subjective life experience studies to comprehensively understand the intricate connection between tourism development and subjective well-being across diverse global contexts.

The Nexus Complexities

In this section, I will explore various relationship types and shapes, elucidating the influence of temporal dynamics, income levels, and critical mediators that impact these relationships, such as economic development, social comparison, and agency. To provide a comprehensive contextual background, I will draw upon insights from countries spanning Central America, South America, the Caribbean, the Mediterranean, Eastern Europe, and Asia.

The results of several studies provide persuasive insights into the dynamic interaction between tourism development and well-being across varied geographical settings. For instance, in a thorough analysis led by Manuel Vanegas and myself, spanning seven Central American nations — Belize, Guatemala, Honduras, El Salvador, Costa Rica, Nicaragua, and Panama

— using annual data from 1995 to 2008, a clear positive correlation between tourism development and well-being was evident. Moreover, a detailed investigation I did into Costa Rica and Nicaragua, employing annual data from 1990 to 2009, reinforced this favorable relationship.

Collaborative research efforts, such as the study conducted in Aruba by myself alongside colleagues Ridderstaat and Nijkamp, revealed similar affirmative findings, highlighting the beneficial impact of tourism development on overall well-being. This investigation, spanning from 1972 to 2011, underscores the enduring nature of this relationship. Expanding the scope, an analysis conducted in Malta in 2017, considering data from 1988 to 2014, revealed a positive relationship between tourism development and well-being. Similarly, a panel analysis across ten South American countries in 2019, including Colombia, Chile, Peru, Argentina, Brazil, Uruguay, Bolivia, Venezuela, Ecuador, and Paraguay, unveiled a consistently positive correlation between tourism and well-being.

Finally, in a more recent study conducted in 2022 focusing on Malaysia, based on annual data from 1996-2018, the results echoed the broader trend observed across various regions, with a discernible positive relationship between tourism and well-being. This reaffirms the complex, impactful nexus between tourism development and overall societal well-being. The comprehensive array of studies conducted in various global contexts provides valuable insights into the relationship between tourism development and well-being.

These studies shed light on the intricate bidirectional relationship between tourism and well-being. This dynamic interaction unveils a symbiotic relationship, yielding mutual benefits for both domains. Take, for instance, the case of Costa Rica. Here, a thriving tourism industry not only drives economic growth but also enriches the overall well-being of its populace through employment opportunities, infrastructure advancements, and cultural enrichment. Conversely, Costa Ricans' heightened sense of well-being cultivates a welcoming atmosphere for tourists, consequently stimulating further growth in the tourism sector. Notably, Costa Rica, boasting a Human Development Index (HDI) of 0.819 and relatively low inequality (with a Gini coefficient of 47.2 in 2022 compared to other Latin American countries), strategically promotes itself as a destination by leveraging well-being as a tourism resource, blending happiness with sustainability consciousness.

Similarly, in Aruba, the correlation between tourism development and well-being highlights how investments in tourism infrastructure and promotion can elevate living standards and enhance the quality of life for residents. This positive association fosters a favorable reputation for the destination as a happy place, attracting more visitors and catalyzing further tourism growth. The concept of "One Happy Island" serves as a potent tourism asset, showcasing and amplifying the reciprocal nature of this relationship. Ultimately, these instances illustrate how the symbiotic bond between tourism development and well-being transcends geographical boundaries, emphasizing the diverse advantages of nurturing a harmonious coexistence between these realms. The following section reveals the intricate and complex relationship between tourism development and well-being viewed through a time warp.

Temporal Nexus Effects

Next, I will explore the short- and long-term effects within the context of the relationship between tourism and well-being. My research delineates the temporal dimension of this relationship using the concept of the output gap, distinguishing between long-term trends and short-term cycles. Short-term effects refer to significant impacts observed over relatively brief durations, ranging from months to several years. For instance, a surge in tourist arrivals during peak seasons may generate short-term economic growth and provide residents with employment opportunities.

Short-term relationships between tourism and well-being can be observed where seasonal tourism spikes lead to immediate economic benefits for local communities. For instance, in coastal destinations, a surge in tourist arrivals during the summer months may result in increased revenue for small businesses, temporary job opportunities in hospitality sectors, and heightened economic activity. Likewise, wellness retreats or spa tourism initiatives can provide short-term boosts to local well-being by offering relaxation and rejuvenation experiences for visitors, contributing to a sense of vitality within the community during their stay.

The case study of Malta illuminates how the link between tourism and well-being can vary significantly over time. While short-term effects might be positive, the long-term impact diverges. Surprisingly, tourism doesn't notably boost economic growth in the long run, possibly due to limited productivity within the tourism industry. This lack of long-term economic impact also ripples into well-being. Interestingly, tourism development initially significantly negatively affects well-being, albeit at a 10% significance level. However, this effect gradually diminishes and could even reverse over time, thanks to its convex nature, as indicated by its squared variable's positive and significant coefficient.

However, the sustainability of any benefits over time necessitates ongoing investment and strategic planning to address potential fluctuations and ensure long-term viability. Long-term effects, however, encompass enduring trends and impacts that unfold gradually over extended periods. These may include the establishment of infrastructure, the cultivation of a positive destination image, and the development of a robust tourism ecosystem. Understanding both short and long-term dynamics is essential for crafting effective policies and strategies that foster sustainable tourism development while maximizing the well-being of residents and visitors.

Conversely, long-term relationships denote enduring associations that evolve over extended periods, shaping broader socio-economic and environmental dynamics. A well-established tourism industry, supported by robust infrastructure and effective destination management, can generate sustained benefits for local economies and cultural preservation efforts. For instance, investments in education and healthcare fueled by tourism revenues can contribute to long-term improvements in public health and human capital development, fostering lasting societal well-being. By examining both short-term fluctuations and long-term trends, policymakers can develop informed strategies to promote inclusive and sustainable tourism development, balancing immediate economic gains with long-term societal and environmental resilience.

Threshold Effects

These findings prompt a crucial inquiry: Is the favorable link between tourism growth and well-being enduring in the long haul, or might there be a tipping point where this connection wanes or reverses? Alternatively, could we witness an initial downturn and an eventual upswing akin to a U-shaped effect? Within tourism discourse, scholars frequently discuss this as a non-linear relationship, suggesting that the advantages of tourism development may plateau rather than perpetually ascend. The implications of these findings are profound, sparking a fundamental question: Can we rely on the enduring correlation between tourism expansion and well-being, or is there a juncture where this bond weakens or flips? Could we experience an initial decline only to see a subsequent rise reminiscent of a U-shaped pattern?

This discussion delves into the heart of tourism discourse, where scholars often grapple with the notion of a non-linear relationship. Here, it is proposed that the benefits of tourism development might not endlessly escalate but could instead reach a point of stabilization, suggesting a plateau effect rather than an indefinite ascent. This perspective adds complexity to our understanding of how tourism influences overall well-being, challenging conventional linear models and prompting a reevaluation of long-term sustainability in tourism planning and development strategies.

One explanation for this non-linear relationship is rooted in the concept of the Dutch disease[46], or what is colloquially referred to as the beach disease.[47] The Dutch disease theory posits that an influx of revenue from a particular sector, such as tourism, can adversely affect other sectors of the economy, such as manufacturing or agriculture. This occurs when the rapid growth of the tourism industry results in currency appreciation, making other exports less competitive on the global market. Consequently, this can lead to economic imbalances, inflationary pressures, and a loss of economic diversification, ultimately undermining long-term economic stability and well-being.

Furthermore, the notion of the beach disease highlights the potential social and environmental consequences of over-reliance on tourism as a primary economic driver. Overdevelopment of coastal areas for tourism purposes and inadequate infrastructure and environmental management can lead to environmental degradation, loss of cultural authenticity, and social dislocation for local communities. As a result, while tourism may initially contribute positively to well-being, unchecked growth without sustainable planning and management strategies can exacerbate inequalities and degrade overall societal welfare over time.

Our research highlights the relatively modest progress of tourism development in South America, with only a select few destinations demonstrating a consistent interaction between tourism and well-being. Instead, we observe a continuous ebb and flow, with periods of strong correlation alternating with instances of weakened connection. This relationship is symbiotic, meaning that tourism competitiveness and human development progress in tandem, each exerting influence on and being influenced by the other. This ongoing interdependence characterizes the dynamic nature of the relationship between tourism competitiveness and human development.

---

[46] See Croes, R. (2022). *Small Island and small destination tourism. Overcoming the smallness barrier for economic growth and tourism competitiveness.* Apple Academic Press: Waretown, NJ, USA.
[47] Holzner M (2011) Tourism and economic development: the beach disease? *Tourism Management* 32(4): 922–933.

Moreover, this intricate interplay may be influenced by threshold effects, shedding light on the regression observed in Venezuela. This dynamic hints at an evolving landscape where the equilibrium between tourism expansion and societal welfare experiences continual fluctuations over time. Particularly noteworthy is the case of Poland, which adds a layer of complexity by showcasing the correlation between tourism development and well-being in a U-shaped trajectory. This implies a pivotal moment where the initial adverse effects of tourism on well-being may diminish and eventually become positive over time.

Our thorough investigation guided us through the intricate interplay shaping the nexus of tourism development and well-being. However, what unfolds is a rich tapestry of complexities that underscore the nuanced essence of this relationship. For instance, in our scrutiny of Aruba, we find evidence pointing to a symbiotic and enduring association between tourism and well-being over the long haul. Conversely, our analysis of Malta and Poland paints a more convoluted picture, revealing that this long-term bond needs to be more straightforward. Indeed, both cases present a compelling narrative of a U-shaped relationship, where the initial impact of tourism development appears negative but gradually transforms into a positive force. This dynamic underscores the multifaceted interplay between tourism and well-being, challenging simplistic linear narratives. It prompts us to question conventional wisdom and delve deeper into the underlying mechanisms driving these shifts.

For instance, in a study conducted by Manuel Rivera and myself in Ecuador, we discovered that despite efforts to promote human development and well-being, the correlation with economic growth remained tenuous. This indicates an imbalance in human development in Ecuador, characterized by stagnant job opportunities. Despite residents possessing requisite skills for the job market, more employment options were needed. The Ecuador case echoes the overarching trend observed in our study across the ten South American countries.

The results of our empirical exploration into the relationship between tourism development and well-being across various geographical contexts carry significant implications that merit careful consideration. Identifying dynamic patterns, wherein the strength of the relationship between tourism and well-being fluctuates over time, highlights the need for a more nuanced understanding of the factors influencing this dynamic. Factors such as economic conditions, policy interventions, institutional strength, agency, cultural dynamics, and environmental sustainability initiatives may all play crucial roles in shaping the trajectory of this relationship. Moreover, the observation of non-linear patterns, such as the case of Malta, underscores the potential for diminishing returns or unintended consequences associated with unchecked tourism expansion. This suggests that while tourism may initially contribute positively to societal well-being, there may exist tipping points where further growth leads to diminishing benefits or even adverse impacts on local communities and the environment.

The case of Malta, with its observed non-linear relationship between tourism and well-being, highlights the potential pitfalls of uncontrolled tourism expansion. Rapid tourism growth may initially stimulate economic development and job creation. However, over time, issues such as environmental degradation, cultural erosion, and social inequality may emerge, leading to diminishing returns regarding societal well-being. Happiness rises with income until a certain threshold, which weakens the connection. External factors and social context influence an individual's happiness, with others' choices impacting their well-being. Constant competition for social status within peer groups may lead to heightened stress and a decline in individual well-being. Pursuing higher social standing through materialism and inequality can restrict opportunities, foster discontent, and amplify unhappiness, emphasizing the impact of social comparisons on perceptions of success and accomplishment in life.

The life cycle of a destination shapes the intricate relationship between tourism development and overall well-being. From initial exploration to maturity and decline, tourism's impacts evolve, ranging from economic opportunities to potential strains on natural resources and social structures. Sustainable tourism practices are crucial to mitigating adverse effects, requiring proactive approaches and effective destination management. Challenges in the decline phase, such as over-dependence on tourism, call for adaptive strategies to revitalize and restore well-being. Proactive and sustainable tourism planning is vital at every stage, ensuring economic thriving while preserving the unique identity and fostering residents' well-being.

Ultimately, the destination life cycle may stem from micro-behavior such as adaptation and social comparison. Economic theory posits that higher income enables individuals to ascend to a higher indifference curve, enhancing utility. However, empirical evidence on the correlation between self-reported life satisfaction (happiness) and income presents a paradoxical scenario. While wealthier nations tend to exhibit higher levels of happiness compared to their less affluent counterparts, individuals with higher incomes typically report greater happiness within each country than those with lower incomes. Nevertheless, analyses spanning several decades reveal a need for significant improvement in self-reported satisfaction levels in many developed countries despite sustained per capita income growth.

Two theories emerge to elucidate this paradox: adaptation and social comparison. The adaptation theory suggests that while an increase in income may initially boost happiness, individuals tend to acclimate to their higher income over time, leading their happiness levels to regress toward their original state. Complete adaptation implies that to maintain the same level of happiness, current income growth must match that of previous years. Conversely, social comparison theory posits that individuals do not evaluate their lives in isolation but rather compare their income and achievements with those of their peers or reference groups. Consequently, an increase in one's peer group's income may engender dissatisfaction, thereby diminishing one's overall life satisfaction. Thus, social comparison theory contends that relative income, rather than absolute income, is the primary determinant of life satisfaction. We will examine these micro-behaviors in the following sections.

The Impact of Income

In exploring the intricate relationship between tourism development and economic growth, I addressed two perspectives shaping well-being. The first perspective zooms in on the individual level, scrutinizing how income impacts people's well-being. Conversely, the second perspective examines the influence of GDP on well-being, considering Richard Easterlin's notion that increased income may not necessarily translate into greater happiness, as evidenced by the Easterlin paradox. This paradox underscores the role of the hedonic treadmill and social comparison, driven by escalating aspirations and comparison effects.

Central to this inquiry was income's critical role as a foundational element in empowering individuals to pursue opportunities for well-being. Initially, my examination focused on tourism's potential to stimulate economic activities and foster growth. To deepen this understanding, I investigated whether economic growth's benefits solely manifest at the macro level or directly translate into improvements in household welfare, prompting two interconnected questions: the influence of tourism on macroeconomic indicators and its implications for household and individual well-being.

In a systematic exploration, I forged a coherent connection between tourism and economic advancement, unraveling the nuanced interplay between these crucial elements. Drawing on trade theories and the Tourism-Led Growth Theory (TLGT) as guiding frameworks, my research sought to solidify the correlation between tourism and economic progress.[48] Through empirical methodologies, I examined macroeconomic indicators alongside micro-level ramifications, shedding light on the intricate mechanisms through which tourism shapes income, employment opportunities, and overall societal well-being on both aggregate and individual scales. Across various case studies encompassing

[48] Croes, R. & Marsiglio, S. (2022). Tourism in an Open System: What Do Theories of International Trade and Competition Teach Us? In Croes, R. & Yang, Y. (2022). (eds.) *A modern guide to tourism economics*. Edward Elgar Publishing: Cheltenham, UK.

Aruba, Malta, Costa Rica, Nicaragua, Malaysia, and Poland, compelling evidence emerged of the symbiotic relationship between tourism and economic development, prompting an exploration into the channels fostering this symbiosis.

The impact of tourism development on well-being is intricately tied to the nature of income distribution — whether it flows through private or public channels. A prime example is Malta, where the source of income notably influences the quality of well-being. Rather than solely focusing on the size of tourism receipts to drive economic growth, examining how these receipts are generated is crucial. Suppose tourism specialization primarily boosts household incomes through human capital, but there is uncertainty about its correlation with economic growth. In that case, it prompts an exploration into the various dynamics of tourism shaping this scenario. In Malta, three dynamics stand out: the attraction of low-value-added content targeting unsuitable tourist segments, a rise in remittances from foreign workers that could stifle local economic growth by depressing wages and purchasing power, and an abundance of part-time jobs due to seasonal fluctuations.[49]

In our examination of Malta and Poland, a striking revelation emerges: The strength and nature of the bond between tourism and well-being hinge heavily on how revenues from tourism are allocated between public coffers and households. This observation leads to a crucial inference: The efficacy of tourism in alleviating poverty is intricately tied to intentional allocations of public income towards poverty reduction initiatives. Essentially, the key lies in how governments allocate and utilize their resources.

A deeper dive into this issue uncovers a profound insight: Household income, while undoubtedly important, exhibits a less direct correlation with two vital pillars of well-being, namely health and education, as

---

[49] Croes, R., Van Niekerk, M., & Ridderstaat, J. (2018). Tourism specialization and quality of life: Evidence from Malta. *Tourism Management, 68*, 212-223.

elucidated by the Human Development Index (HDI). This revelation underscores the pivotal role of public resources in shaping these essential aspects of human welfare. Factors such as life expectancy, a critical indicator of well-being, are profoundly influenced by the adequacy of and access to healthcare and the quality of education, primarily driven by public expenditures rather than individual household spending.

Enter tourism is a dynamic force that generates employment, wages, and income and yields substantial tax revenue for governments. This revenue, in turn, becomes the lifeblood of public expenditures, funding crucial investments in human development. Nowhere is this dynamic more pronounced than in smaller island nations like Malta, where government spending assumes a paramount role in bolstering healthcare and education, dwarfing the influence of household expenditures. Thus, tourism's significance transcends mere economic gains; it lies in the equitable distribution of these benefits across society and the degree to which its growth reinforces public services. By recognizing the pivotal interplay between tourism revenue, public expenditure, and human development, policymakers can chart a course toward a more inclusive and sustainable future where tourism's dividends enrich all citizens' lives, regardless of socioeconomic status.

The study on tourism's impact on well-being in Poland underscores two central propositions. The first proposition highlights the significance of private income from tourism in bolstering human development. The second one features the indispensable role of public goods and resources supporting a prudent allocation strategy. Acknowledging potential disparities in access to goods and services, the study emphasizes the need for a nuanced understanding of the interplay between private and public resources in promoting well-being through tourism. Similarly, the critical role of government and institutional frameworks in advancing well-being through tourism initiatives is highlighted, signaling the importance of resource utilization. Subsequently, a more profound exploration into the specific roles governments and institutions play in this realm is warranted.

Moreover, a comprehensive analysis spanning ten South American nations underscores a direct correlation between the expansion of tourism and the enhancement of societal capabilities. For instance, when examining the average receipts from tourism, it becomes evident that they positively influence access to crucial resources like healthcare and education. This correlation initiates a constructive feedback loop: As tourism receipts escalate, governments find themselves endowed with greater financial resources for fortifying public services. Consequently, this allocation leads to tangible enhancements in these essential services' overall quality and availability. The ripple effects are profound: Improved access to healthcare and education uplifts individual well-being and catalyzes societal development and prosperity, rendering destinations more appealing to prospective visitors.

In a joint study led by Manuel Vanegas and me, our research delved into the tourism sectors of Costa Rica, Guatemala, and the Dominican Republic. Our findings highlighted a significant barrier to realizing the full potential of tourism resources in driving economic growth and improving well-being: inequality. We discovered that despite the considerable resources directed toward tourism, the benefits of poverty reduction and overall well-being were hindered by existing disparities. In essence, our study underscored that addressing underlying inequalities is necessary for any positive impact of tourism on well-being, at best. This suggests that initiatives aimed at reducing inequality must be integrated into tourism development strategies to unlock its full potential in fostering inclusive growth and improving the lives of local communities.

However, tourism income's impact on individual well-being can vary significantly because well-being is profoundly personal and cannot be fully captured by objective measures like income and jobs. These traditional metrics may affect people differently. Personal values and circumstances unique to each influence the link between income and well-being. As Sen suggests, people's ability to convert resources like income into well-being varies. My research shows that while tourism can increase income, it only sometimes enhances well-being. For example, in Aruba, higher income didn't strongly correlate with greater happiness, and factors like social comparison significantly impacted residents' happiness.[50] Similarly, in Sopot, adaptation biases obscured the income-happiness connection.[51] Therefore, relying solely on objective conditions to assess well-being can lead to interpretation. Incorporating subjective measures of well-being may provide a better understanding of the relationship between tourism development and well-being.

Government, Agency and Social Comparison

In collaboration with colleagues at Rosen College, the University of South Carolina, and the University of Gdansk, two studies explored the intricate role of government, agency, and social comparison. The initial research, centered on tourism and well-being within the Malaysian context, utilized government and agency as mediators in the relationship between tourism and well-being.[52] It was observed that for destinations and government officials, the performance of tourism plays a pivotal role in garnering support from residents for further developmental endeavors, contingent upon the perceived benefits of tourism to residents. However, inherent market distortions and individual agency might impede the equitable distribution of these benefits. These distortions often stem from prevailing social arrangements and governance structures, such as

---

[50] See, for example, Ridderstaat, J., Croes, R., & Nijkamp, P. (2016). A two-way causal chain between tourism development and quality of life in a small island destination: An empirical analysis. *Journal of Sustainable Tourism*, 24 (10), 1461-1479; and Rivera, M., Croes, R., & Lee, S. (2016). Tourism development and happiness: A residents' perspective. *Journal of Destination Marketing & Management*, 5(1), 5-15.

[51] See Croes, R., Shapoval, V., Rivera, M., Bak, M. & Zientara, P. (2024). Promoting Residents' Happiness Through a Human-Centric Approach to Tourism City Development. *International Journal of Tourism Cities*, https://doi.org/10.1108/IJTC-05-2023-0105.

[52] Croes, R., Kubickova, M. & Ridderstaat, J. (2022). Destination competitiveness and human development: the compelling critical force of human agency. *Journal of Hospitality and Tourism Research*, https://doi.org/10.1177/10963480221140022.

unemployment and inadequate access to financial resources, potentially leading to deprivation and a limitation of human agency.

Human agency, as posited by Amartya Sen, Nobel Prize in Economic Sciences in 1998 for his contributions to welfare economics, plays a crucial role in this context, as it denotes the capacity of individuals to effect change through their actions, either individually or collectively. These actions are shaped by personal motivations, capabilities, social pressures, and public policies, reflecting a dynamic interaction between behavior, environment, and outcomes. Sen's framework suggests that disparities in access to resources and social roles influence individuals' actions, impacting their well-being and societal integration. Additionally, contextual mechanisms significantly mediate the relationship between tourism and residents' human development, affecting the realization of capabilities such as good health, self-respect, and happiness.

Furthermore, the Malaysia study highlights the intrinsic link between agency and governance, wherein societal arrangements can either facilitate or hinder the activation and realization of individual capabilities. Notably, the study underscores the pivotal role of human agency in shaping the reciprocal relationship between tourism and human development, aligning with the central tenets of the capability approach. Surprisingly, the study found a need for a more significant impact of governance on this relationship in the Malaysian context. This finding raises important questions about the underlying dynamics at play. Factors such as weak institutional capacity, corruption, and policy fragmentation may contribute to this phenomenon. Additionally, persistent inequalities and limited public participation in governance processes could further hinder the translation of tourism competitiveness into meaningful improvements in human well-being for all segments of society.

Despite Malaysia's impressive economic growth trajectory, facilitated by government interventions and policies aimed at inclusive development, challenges persist, particularly concerning political stability. The country's average score for political stability, as measured from 1996 to 2018, remains below average, impacting social connectedness and economic diversification efforts. These challenges, often called conversion factors by Sen, influence various aspects of well-being, including occupational choices, opportunities, and social inclusion.

Moreover, while Malaysia's tourism sector boasts a respectable ranking according to the Travel and Tourism Competitiveness Index, it faces weaknesses in areas such as health, sustainability, and tourist service infrastructure, particularly amid the ongoing COVID-19 pandemic and increasing concerns about climate change. Addressing these issues necessitates a comprehensive approach considering the interplay between governance, agency, and societal arrangements to foster sustainable and inclusive development in Malaysia's tourism sector.

The interplay between agency, tourism, and well-being in Central American countries reveals a complex dynamic. Through our research, my colleagues and I unearthed a significant adverse effect of human agency on well-being. At the core of this discovery lies the persistent issue of unmet needs within the region, which, unfortunately, is normalized. This widespread deprivation is evidenced by the prevalence of poverty, inequality, exclusion, violence, and crime, all of which hinder individuals from fulfilling their necessities. Compounding this challenge needs more institutional support to tackle these issues effectively. Instances of inadequate protection of citizens' property and labor rights serve as stark reminders of the shortcomings of governance in Central America, as highlighted by dismal scores in economic freedom indices. Drawing from Sen's capability approach, where agency plays a pivotal role, we observe a dichotomy between active agency, exemplified by countries like Malaysia, and passive agency, which is characteristic of Central American nations.

Turning to the role of social comparison as a mediator in the relationship between tourism and well-being. Recognizing our innate inclination toward social comparison, the study about Sopot highlights how inequality acts as a magnifier, potentially dampening the anticipated gains in well-being from increased incomes spurred by tourism.[53] While tourism generates private and public incomes that can enhance utility and capabilities, the study underscores that individual happiness cannot be solely measured by income. While an initial rise in income correlates with increased happiness as basic needs are met, pursuing higher income becomes intertwined with fulfilling higher-level psychological needs. This complexity suggests that the correlation between income and happiness plateaus after a point, with aspirations for growth influenced by social status, potentially curbing opportunities and amplifying unhappiness.

The study emphasizes the subjective nature of well-being, which is influenced by individuals' perceptions and responses to external conditions, particularly those affecting their social ranking. Social comparison processes play a significant role in shaping subjective well-being as individuals assess their success relative to others. Drawing on behavioral economics, the Sopot study hypothesizes that tourism contributes to residents' happiness through social comparison, linking happiness with subjective evaluations of external circumstances.

The study employs a subjective well-being approach to examine the impact of social comparison in the case of Sopot, Poland. Surprisingly, despite Sopot's high Human Development Index (HDI), which indicates overall well-being, the analysis reveals unfulfilled basic needs among residents, attributed to escalating income inequality in the region. The stark contrast between reported life satisfaction and happiness levels underscores the reality of income inequality, suggesting that fundamental needs such as housing, healthcare, and education may not be adequately addressed despite the economic development associated with city tourism.

Furthermore, the study suggests that the relationship between tourism development factors and happiness is mediated by comparisons of life situations. Tourism's social and environmental domains notably

---

[53] Croes, R., Shapoval, V., Rivera, M., Bak, M. & Zientara, P. (2024). Promoting Residents' Happiness Through a Human-Centric Approach to Tourism City Development. *International Journal of Tourism Cities*, https://doi.org/10.1108/IJTC-05-2023-0105.

exhibit significant adverse impacts, possibly due to rising aspirations and comparison effects. Residents may gauge their well-being by comparing their living standards to those of their peers, which may lead to dissatisfaction if disparities are perceived. Additionally, heightened expectations fueled by visible improvements brought about by tourism may contrast negatively with residents' current living standards, impacting their perceived happiness. This underscores the intricate interplay of social dynamics and environmental considerations in shaping residents' well-being within the tourism context.

Social comparison emerged as a prominent theme in our research, which was conducted in Aruba and several other islands across the Caribbean region. In these studies, we delved into the intricate dynamics of how individuals in these island communities perceive their well-being relative to others, particularly concerning the influence of tourism development. In Aruba and various other Caribbean islands, tourism plays a pivotal role in shaping the local economy and society. Tourism flourishes and brings forth economic opportunities, infrastructure development, and cultural exchanges. However, alongside these benefits, tourism development often triggers social comparisons among residents.

Residents may compare their living standards, opportunities, and social status with others within their community or even tourists visiting their island. These social comparisons can affect individuals' perceptions of their well-being. On the one hand, witnessing the prosperity and affluence associated with tourism may inspire aspirations for a better life and drive individuals to strive for improvement. On the other hand, disparities in wealth and opportunities may lead to feelings of inadequacy or resentment, particularly if individuals perceive themselves as falling short compared to others.

Moreover, social comparison dynamics can extend beyond economic considerations to encompass various aspects of well-being, including social relationships, cultural identity, and environmental stewardship. For instance, residents may compare their social interactions, community cohesion, and sense of belonging with those of other residents or tourists. Similarly, they may assess the preservation of their cultural heritage and natural environment compared to other destinations or past conditions.

Understanding the role of social comparison in tourism development is crucial for policymakers, community leaders, and stakeholders involved in shaping the trajectory of these island economies. By acknowledging and addressing the implications of social comparisons, interventions can be designed to foster inclusive growth, promote social cohesion, and enhance residents' overall well-being. This may involve initiatives to reduce income inequality, provide equitable access to resources and opportunities, and foster a sense of pride and ownership among residents in the benefits of tourism development.

Wrapping Up

The chapter provides an insightful analysis of the complex relationship between tourism development and well-being, drawing upon diverse case studies and empirical investigations across various geographic contexts. By scrutinizing the interplay between income, economic growth, and subjective well-being, the chapter navigated through the intricacies of this relationship, shedding light on both the positive associations and potential challenges. Through systematic exploration guided by theoretical frameworks such as the Tourism-Led Growth Theory (TLGT) and insights from trade theories, the research underscores the symbiotic relationship between tourism and economic development, highlighting the channels through which tourism shapes income, employment opportunities, and societal well-being.

Moreover, the analysis extends beyond the macroeconomic realm to delve into micro-level ramifications, revealing tangible enhancements in access to crucial resources such as healthcare and education catalyzed by tourism-driven economic growth. However, underlying disparities and inequalities pose significant barriers to realizing the full potential of tourism resources in driving inclusive growth and improving well-being, emphasizing the imperative of addressing structural inequalities in tourism development strategies.

The role of government, agency, and social comparison emerges as central themes in understanding the complex interplay between tourism development and well-being. By elucidating how societal arrangements, governance structures, and individual agency shape this relationship, the study underscores the importance of a nuanced understanding of these factors in fostering sustainable and inclusive tourism development. Social comparison dynamics further illuminate the subjective nature of well-being within the tourism context, emphasizing the implications of income inequality and disparities on residents' perceptions of happiness and life satisfaction.

The analysis of the relationship between tourism development and well-being illuminates several vital conditions that shape the complex interplay between these two phenomena. Geographical context emerges as a fundamental factor, with regional variations influencing how tourism impacts well-being worldwide. The examination of diverse case studies from regions such as the Caribbean, Mediterranean, South America, Eastern Europe, and Asia underscores the nuanced nature of this relationship, emphasizing the need for context-specific approaches to policy interventions.

Furthermore, temporal dynamics, income levels, and mediators like economic development, social comparison, and agency are crucial in shaping the *tourism and well-being* nexus. The bidirectional nature of this relationship highlights how tourism not only enhances societal well-being but also derives momentum from improved well-being, suggesting a symbiotic dynamic that evolves. Moreover, the analysis delves into the micro-level implications of tourism development, revealing tangible enhancements in access to essential resources such as healthcare and education. However, underlying disparities and inequalities pose significant challenges, underscoring the importance of addressing structural inequalities to ensure equitable distribution of the benefits of tourism development.

At the macroeconomic level, income distribution, both through private and public channels, emerges as a critical factor influencing the impact of tourism on household welfare and overall societal well-being. Equitable resource allocation and the role of government in fostering inclusive growth are critical determinants of the extent to which tourism development translates into improved well-being for host communities. The examination of empirical methodologies and case studies further underscores the importance of addressing underlying disparities and inequalities to fully harness the potential of tourism as a driver of inclusive growth.

Additionally, the role of government, agency, and social comparison dynamics in shaping the *tourism and well-being* relationship highlights the need for a nuanced understanding of societal arrangements and governance structures. By fostering sustainable and inclusive tourism development, policymakers and stakeholders can leverage tourism as a catalyst for societal advancement, thereby enhancing the well-being of both residents and visitors alike. The comprehensive analysis provides valuable insights into the intricate relationship between tourism development and well-being, offering a roadmap for designing holistic approaches that prioritize inclusive growth, equitable resource distribution, and social cohesion.

A Semblance of Coherence

IN THIS FINAL CHAPTER, I EMBARK ON A REFLECTIVE JOURNEY through the depths of my research expedition. Herein lies a synthesis of my experiences, insights gained, and a roadmap for future endeavors. As I look back on my research odyssey, I am compelled to trace the Daedalian pathways that have led me to this culminating moment. Each twist and turn, every discovery and setback, has sculpted the narrative of my scholarly voyage. Through painstaking inquiry and unwavering dedication, I have traversed the terrain of knowledge, uncovering hidden truths and probing the boundaries of understanding about tourism and well-being.

Yet, not merely the destinations reached define this journey, but the lessons gleaned along the way. Writing this book taught me about the gripping dynamics of the relationship between tourism and well-being, uncovering a tapestry woven with socioeconomic disparities, cultural nuances, and institutional influences. Central to this exploration is the aspiration and expectation gaps that underscore the importance of addressing socio-economic inequalities in access to travel opportunities. Moreover, I have learned that adaptability plays a pivotal role in shaping individuals' experiences, highlighting the need for inclusive practices that cater to diverse needs and backgrounds. Furthermore, recognizing institutional and systemic barriers has reinforced the imperative of promoting equitable access to travel resources and infrastructure. Ultimately, this journey has emphasized the transformative potential of responsible and inclusive tourism practices in fostering well-being and enhancing the travel experience for all individuals and communities involved.

My Research Journey

My research paradigm shifted when I made a conscious decision to move beyond the narrow confines of rationality and self-interest when exploring the intricate relationship between tourism development and well-being. Realizing the limitations of traditional utility theories, which predominantly focus on individual preferences and satisfaction, I embraced a more holistic perspective anchored in human development and capability.

The human development framework, unlike linear models, introduced a cyclical process involving inputs, conversion factors, process, and outcomes. It highlighted the significance of various inputs in overall well-being, such as education, healthcare, income, and freedom. The conversion factors, including social interactions, policies, and cultural influences, played a pivotal role in determining how (process) these inputs translated into capabilities, ultimately influencing the ability to lead a fulfilling life.

This broader lens allowed me to delve into the complexities of the relationship between tourism development and human development. Acknowledging the multifaceted nature of well-being, the research extended beyond immediate impacts on individuals to consider broader societal implications and long-term outcomes. Recognition of conversion factors became crucial for emphasizing this relationship's nonlinear and context-dependent nature.

As I immersed myself in this exploration, the capability approach emerged as a promising framework. It highlighted the individual's ability to achieve valuable "beings and doings" in life as a measure of well-being, emphasizing the importance of life experiences in understanding one's overall quality of life. This approach introduced the concept of "functionings," encompassing objective aspects like health and education and subjective experiences like happiness and autonomy.

A pivotal turning point in my research came with the realization that life experiences are central to comprehending well-being, surpassing the limitations of traditional measures such as GDP per capita. This insight resonates with the influential Stiglitz Report, formally titled "Report by the Commission on the Measurement of Economic Performance and Social Progress."[54] Commissioned in 2008, the report, led by Nobel laureate economists Joseph Stiglitz, Amartya Sen, and Jean-Paul Fitoussi, addressed the need for more comprehensive economic indicators to measure societal well-being. The report underscored the necessity of a combined approach considering objective and subjective measures to represent well-being accurately. This aligns with the crux of my research, which emphasizes the significance of life experiences in understanding overall satisfaction and quality of life.

Incorporating insights from the Stiglitz Report, my research aimed to balance subjective perceptions with objective indicators. This nuanced measurement approach allowed for a comprehensive evaluation of tourism's impacts on different dimensions of well-being. The debate on objective versus subjective indicators in the broader literature on quality of life further reinforced the importance of considering individual perceptions, aligning with the argument that well-being is inherently subjective and should be measured through open-ended surveys. I understood that a comprehensive understanding of human well-being necessitates the integration of both subjective and objective perspectives. Acknowledging the inherent subjectivity of well-being, shaped by individual circumstances and values, is crucial. However, solely relying on subjective well-being metrics risks succumbing to the Senian notion of

[54] Stiglitz, J.M., Sen, A. & Fitoussi, J. (2009). *Report by the commission on the measurement of economic performance and social progress.* Paris: Commission on the measurement of economic performance and social progress. Retrieved January 6, 2024 from http://www.stiglitz-sen-fitoussi.fr/documents/rapport_anglais.pdf.

hedonic adaptation, potentially skewing policy decisions based on fleeting snapshots of societal progress.

Well-being extends beyond subjective experiences to encompass achievements, opportunities, and the freedom to pursue them. The distribution and availability of resources significantly influence well-being. Thus, it is essential to question how different societal resource allocations can contribute to a fulfilling life and whether specific resource categories, particularly those linked to tourism development, like environmental, cultural, and material resources, might clash.[55] Resources, whether income or non-income, such as agency, serve as critical conversion factors enabling meaningful pursuits and states of being. However, integrating evaluation with achievements, such as Senian functionings, must be clarified. By bridging this complexity, researchers and policymakers can develop interventions that enhance individuals' overall well-being.

Moreover, while the insights derived from well-being research are invaluable, a cautious approach is necessary in translating these findings into policy interventions. One-size-fits-all approaches risk oversimplification and may overlook individuals' and communities' diverse needs and perspectives. For instance, while cross-sectional analyses often emphasize indicators like life satisfaction or happiness, they frequently disregard the broader values that residents and tourists prioritize, such as health, education, income, social connections, and cultural richness. This oversight limits the depth of analysis, as cross-sectional approaches typically provide correlations without facilitating inferential insights. In essence, navigating the intricate landscape of tourism and quality of life underscores the importance of a nuanced understanding for crafting effective policies and interventions. By delving deeper into the complexities of resource allocation, societal values, individual aspirations, and opportunities, we can forge pathways toward

---

[55] See, for example, Croes, R., Shapoval, V., Rivera, M., Bak, M. & Zientara, P. (2024). Promoting Residents' Happiness Through a Human-Centric Approach to Tourism City Development. *International Journal of Tourism Cities*, https://doi.org/10.1108/IJTC-05-2023-0105.

sustainable development and enhanced well-being for all stakeholders within the tourism ecosystem.

In future research on tourism and well-being, several additional factors deserve attention. Exploring the conditions that help or hinder quality of life is crucial, especially regarding how society allocates and distributes resources. For example, examining how fair decision-making processes and equitable resource distribution impact community happiness can reveal important insights. Studies show that fairness and equity play key roles in boosting happiness. Using Sen's concepts of positional objectivity (how people's positions in society affect their views) and relational capability (how social relationships affect well-being), researchers can better understand and address issues that might divide communities.

Additionally, it is essential to consider whose subjective well-being is being measured. Should our research include perspectives from Indigenous peoples, individuals with disabilities, and children? Including these often-overlooked groups can provide valuable insights into the different aspects of well-being within diverse communities. This inclusive approach not only broadens the scope of research but also leads to a deeper understanding of what influences well-being across various demographic segments.

For instance, research could look at how tourism development affects the well-being of indigenous communities, considering their unique cultural and environmental connections. Similarly, studies might investigate how accessible tourism impacts individuals with disabilities or how tourism affects children in terms of educational opportunities and social development. By incorporating these diverse perspectives, we can develop more comprehensive and effective policies that enhance the well-being of all members of society.

Incorporating the capability approach into my research marked a significant departure from traditional economic theories that often prioritize material aspects in assessing development and well-being. The capability approach, championed by Amartya Sen and Martha Nussbaum, broadens the scope beyond GDP-centric measures and emphasizes the inherent diversity in individuals' abilities to lead fulfilling lives. This diversity is intricately tied to the social, economic, and political environments that shape individuals' capabilities.

My research revolves around these two key dimensions: material foundations and opportunities and the subjective assessment of well-being. Notably, the scope of my research primarily centers on the residents of destinations, recognizing that the well-being of tourists is an equally significant aspect that can be explored separately within the quality of life and well-being research.[56] The concept of "functionings" within the capability approach underscores the importance of considering various aspects contributing to human well-being. These can include basic needs such as health and education and more intangible and subjective elements like autonomy, social connections, and a sense of purpose. By recognizing the rich nature of human experiences, the capability approach provides a framework for acknowledging the richness and variety of individual lives, thus contributing to a more comprehensive understanding of well-being.

As the research unfolded, it became increasingly apparent that the measurement of well-being is a complex and nuanced task. As highlighted by the Stiglitz Report, the debate between objective and subjective indicators introduced a critical dimension to this challenge. Objective measures, such as GDP per capita, provide a quantitative snapshot but may need to capture the intricacies of individual experiences. On the other hand, subjective measures, derived from individual perceptions and experiences, offer a more personal and qualitative understanding of well-being. The fusion of both approaches, as the Stiglitz Report advocates, enables a more holistic evaluation that considers both the tangible and intangible aspects of human flourishing.

---

[56] See, for example, Uysal, M., Sirgy, M. J., Woo, E., & Kim, H. (L.). (2016). Quality of life (QOL) and well-being research in tourism. *Tourism Management, 53,* 244–261. https://doi.org/10.1016/j.tourman.2015.07.013.

Context matters emerged as a central theme in the research journey. The understanding that the relationship between tourism development and well-being is contingent on specific conditions challenges the traditional inclination towards generalization. Recognizing the role of mediators and moderators within specific contexts emphasizes the need for a nuanced, context-dependent approach. This shift from a rigid theoretical framework to an appreciation of contextual intricacies allows for a more realistic and applicable analysis of the impacts of tourism on human development and capability.

Finally, my research findings underscore several critical dimensions of well-being. Firstly, happiness and satisfaction with life emerge as fundamental pillars of overall well-being, intricately linked yet distinct in their manifestations. While they share a relationship, they possess unique qualities that set them apart. Secondly, inequality emerges as a formidable adversary, capable of eroding the benefits that tourism bestows upon residents. Inequality acts as the kryptonite, thwarting the equitable distribution of tourism-related advantages and impeding inclusive growth. Thirdly, the nuanced impact of social comparison comes to the fore, revealing its complex interplay with economic development and equality. Depending on contextual factors, the effects of social comparison can oscillate between positive and negative trajectories. Understanding these dynamics is crucial for devising effective policies and interventions that foster sustainable development and enhance the well-being of communities affected by tourism.

My research trajectory underwent a paradigm shift, evolving from reductionist perspectives to embracing a more comprehensive, dynamic, and context-sensitive approach. By integrating the capability approach, human development framework, and insights from the Stiglitz Report, the study sought to contribute a richer understanding of how tourism development shapes the diverse dimensions of human well-being. This journey represented a progression from rigid rationality to a more holistic, human-centric approach, aiming for a more inclusive and meaningful assessment of societal progress. In conclusion, informed by the ongoing discourse on well-being measurement, my research aimed to offer a nuanced understanding of the intricate interplay between tourism development and the diverse dimensions of human well-being, encapsulating a transformative shift in perspective.

Ten Lessons

Lesson 1: Happiness as a Universal Endeavor

The research findings shed light on the intricate dynamics surrounding the universal pursuit of happiness, a fundamental aspect of human existence transcending cultural, social, and economic boundaries. While the perspective of Amartya Sen positions happiness as one among many valuable functionings, the accumulated evidence suggests that it is a universal endeavor deeply ingrained in the human experience. It becomes apparent that happiness manifests differently across societies and individuals, yet it remains a common thread weaving through the fabric of human existence. This understanding prompts a reevaluation of happiness not merely as a subjective emotion but as a fundamental aspect of human flourishing, deserving attention and consideration in various spheres of life.

Moreover, the research underscores the broad nature of happiness, revealing its intricate connections with social relationships, familial bonds, and various aspects of life. While aspirations and capabilities undoubtedly play a role in shaping happiness, the quality of social connections is a significant determinant of individuals' overall well-being. Strong support networks and resilient social ties contribute to individuals' ability to navigate adversity and find fulfillment in their lives. Thus, pursuing happiness is not solely an individual endeavor but is deeply intertwined with the social fabric within which individuals are embedded. The extensive research over a decade has provided profound insights into residents' happiness levels in destination areas, particularly evident in small island destinations like Aruba and the Bahamas. The consistently high happiness scores reported across multiple years suggest the presence of enduring patterns of contentment among inhabitants in these tourism-centric locales.

Complementary studies in other Caribbean islands corroborate these findings, indicating a widespread positive sentiment among residents. Interestingly, these happiness scores closely align with those identified by other scholars, hinting at a potential universality of human well-being transcending cultural and economic boundaries. This finding suggests that despite differences in context, there may be shared fundamental aspects of life satisfaction rooted in universal human needs and aspirations. The case of the Bahamas provides a particularly intriguing example, where respondents' overall happiness scores exceeded their satisfaction with life scores. This nuanced disparity underscores the complexity of subjective well-being, wherein immediate emotional experiences may differ from broader assessments of life satisfaction.

Lesson 2: Aspirations, Capabilities and Expectations Are Not Straightforward

The congruence between aspirations and capabilities in the Bahamas suggests a positive alignment, indicating that individuals are achieving their goals despite potential disparities between their aspirations and perceived capabilities. This insightful perspective highlights the importance of considering various dimensions of well-being to gain a comprehensive understanding of individuals' overall life satisfaction. It underscores the need for tailored approaches to enhancing well-being across diverse contexts.

However, the relationship between happiness, aspirations, and capabilities is more complex and linear but somewhat nuanced and context-dependent. While there may be a positive correlation between these factors under favorable conditions, structural barriers, socioeconomic constraints, and limited resource access can complicate this relationship. In environments marked by inequality and limited opportunities, individuals may struggle to realize their aspirations despite possessing the necessary capabilities, leading to feelings of frustration or discontent. Additionally, unrealistic aspirations without adequate capabilities can contribute to stress and dissatisfaction, highlighting the importance of addressing broader contextual factors to promote sustainable happiness.

In these circumstances, individuals may struggle to realize their aspirations despite possessing the necessary capabilities, leading to feelings of frustration or discontent. Moreover, the pursuit of unrealistic aspirations in the absence of adequate capabilities can also give rise to stress or dissatisfaction. Therefore, while a positive correlation between happiness, aspirations, and capabilities may exist under certain favorable conditions, it is essential to consider the broader contextual factors that shape this relationship.

Lesson 3: The Uneasy Relationship Between Happiness and Social Comparison

Another intriguing lesson from my research is the intricate relationship between happiness and social comparison. What emerges is a nuanced understanding of how various contextual factors, including the stage of development, generational differences, and income distribution within a society, can influence this relationship. In specific contexts, social comparison may fuel upward comparisons, wherein individuals aspire to achieve tremendous success or status relative to their peers, potentially enhancing their happiness and fulfillment.

Conversely, in environments characterized by income inequality or social disparities, social comparison may trigger downward comparisons, leading individuals to feel discontented or inadequate in comparison to others who appear more privileged or successful. Furthermore, generational differences can shape the nature of social comparison, with younger generations often exposed to heightened levels of comparison through social media and digital platforms. Consequently, understanding the nuanced interplay between happiness and social comparison requires a holistic examination of the broader societal context, including economic development, social norms, and cultural values.

Lesson 4: The Role of Income and Generations

The interaction between income and well-being, whether at individual or household levels, reveals the nuanced dynamics of economic progress. While conventional wisdom suggests that higher income leads to greater happiness, the Easterlin paradox challenges this notion, citing factors like the hedonic treadmill and social comparison. Additionally, examining the impact of tourism on broader economic indicators underscores the necessity for a comprehensive understanding of its role in fostering economic development. Income distribution emerges as a critical factor, as seen in Malta and South America studies, where tourism-generated income significantly affects societal well-being, indicating its potential to enhance access to essential services.

Generational differences in happiness in small island communities like Aruba and Curacao reveal complex dynamics shaped by diverse life experiences and societal influences. While Aruba shows consistent happiness across generations, Curacao displays significant disparities. Age-related perspectives contribute to happiness variations, with Curacao experiencing reduced happiness during social comparisons. In contrast, Aruba's unique contextual conditions foster a more consistent happiness experience. Policymakers must consider these dynamics to tailor interventions effectively and promote happiness and life satisfaction in each island community.

Lesson 5: Poverty, Inequality, and Happiness

My research across Latin America also sheds light on the intricate dynamics of subjective well-being amidst challenges like poverty and inequality. Despite economic disparities, respondents from Mexico, Costa Rica, and Ecuador consistently report high happiness levels, possibly due to tight-knit communities and cultural resilience. However, economic gaps affect happiness differently across income brackets and age groups, reflecting societal values' influence. Understanding these nuances is crucial for tailored interventions to address well-being disparities effectively.

Moreover, the study reveals that inequality substantially dampens tourism's positive effects on well-being, presenting a significant obstacle to harnessing tourism for poverty reduction and overall well-being improvement. By addressing underlying inequalities, tourism's transformative potential is unlimited, emphasizing the necessity for integrated strategies prioritizing inclusivity and equitable distribution of benefits.

Additionally, the role of public goods and resources in supporting well-being through tourism initiatives is highlighted, underscoring the importance of prudent allocation strategies and effective governance frameworks to maximize tourism's benefits for well-being enhancement.

Social comparison is crucial in shaping individuals' happiness, and factors like development stage, generational differences, and income distribution influence it. Positive comparisons can boost happiness, but disparities may lead to feelings of inadequacy. Understanding this interplay requires examining societal context, including economic development and cultural values. In Aruba, research shows a positive link between social comparison and happiness, mostly involving upward comparisons. Reduced wealth gaps suggest that movements toward equality empower such comparisons. Policymakers must address social and economic disparities to foster healthier social comparisons and enhance overall well-being.

Lesson 6: The Relationship Between Dynamic Tourism and Well-being

The analysis of various studies across Central America, South America, the Caribbean, the Mediterranean, Eastern Europe, and Asia presents compelling evidence of the complex relationship between tourism development and well-being. From Costa Rica to Aruba and Malaysia, these investigations consistently reveal a positive correlation between tourism and overall societal well-being, emphasizing the enduring nature of this connection across diverse global contexts.

While exceptions like Poland and Malta highlight the need for nuanced understanding, the symbiotic relationship between tourism and well-being is evident. Costa Rica's case illustrates how a flourishing tourism industry enhances economic growth and enriches well-being, while Aruba's "One Happy Island" branding showcases how investments in tourism elevate living standards and attract visitors, creating a growth cycle. These insights underscore the importance of embracing a bidirectional perspective in tourism planning and policymaking to foster sustainable development and inclusive growth that prioritize the well-being of both residents and visitors, transcending geographical boundaries.

Lesson 7: U-shape Relationships

My research reveals the nuanced interaction between tourism and well-being, revealing an evolving and reciprocal feedback loop. Uncovering threshold effects demonstrates an intriguing U-shape pattern, indicating that the relationship is nuanced rather than linear. For example, in Poland, we found that the effect of tourism development on well-being was negative, but the squared version of tourism was positive and statistically significant. This result implies a U-shape relationship, which means that tourism's effect on well-being was at first negative but, beyond a certain threshold, had a positive impact on well-being. We found a similar effect in the case of Malta.

This complexity is compounded by factors such as the source and utilization of tourism-generated income and its influence on household and public income. The association between tourism and well-being is heavily mediated by income, with diminishing effects observed over time. Understanding these dynamics necessitates adaptive strategies and proactive measures to mitigate adverse impacts and foster long-term prosperity. This emphasizes the need for a balanced approach to tourism planning and policy-making that prioritizes sustainable growth and equitable distribution of benefits.

The temporal dimension of the well-being relationship is highlighted, distinguishing between short-term impacts and long-term trends. Short-term effects encompass immediate benefits like economic growth and employment opportunities during peak tourist seasons or targeted wellness initiatives. However, ensuring the sustainability of these benefits requires ongoing investment and strategic planning to address potential fluctuations. Conversely, long-term effects unfold gradually, encompassing infrastructure development, positive destination image cultivation, and a robust tourism ecosystem. Balancing short-term gains with long-term resilience is crucial for crafting policies that promote sustainable tourism development while maximizing well-being benefits for residents and visitors, ultimately ensuring inclusive and environmentally sound growth in the tourism sector.

Lesson 8: The Role of Agency and Government

Within the tourism context, individual agency emerges as a key influencer in shaping perceptions of well-being, with Malaysia serving as a prime example. The capability approach, central to this discourse, emphasizes the crucial role of human agency in this intricate dynamic. Despite notable government interventions such as AIM microfinancing to empower women and address income disparities, governance's impact remains surprisingly limited. The AIM initiative targets opportunities for individuals to enhance their economic status, mitigate risks, and build resilience. Poverty alleviation, encompassing economic stability and access to essential services, gained prominence with the advent of microcredit, championed by Yunus. Microfinance initiatives like Grameen Bank have notably empowered women, enabling them to exert greater control over assets and family decisions.

However, governance's efficacy is constrained by its predominant focus on institutional efficiency, eclipsing broader considerations of individual agency. Sen's concept of agency reinforces a relational understanding of society, wherein the realization of capabilities depends on interactions and societal positions, termed positional objectivity. Governance structures can either facilitate or hinder the activation and fulfillment of agency, influencing access to education, employment, nourishment, self-respect, and happiness. This underscores the need for governance frameworks that prioritize efficiency and empower individuals to exercise agency and realize their full potential within society.

While Malaysia's economic growth trajectory has been impressive, political stability remains a significant concern. Poor political stability adversely affects social connectedness and economic growth potential, hindering the realization of human capabilities and occupational opportunities. Additionally, areas for improvement in Malaysia's tourism sector, especially in health, sustainability, and infrastructure, pose challenges and increasing focus on climate change. Human agency supersedes governance in shaping resource allocation for tourism, emphasizing the importance of empowering individuals through occupational opportunities.

Lesson 9: The Interplay between Context and Concept

My research underscores the pivotal role of context in the cases examined, revealing its significance in theory development. While context initially appears as a barrier to generalizations, it serves as a rich source of observations by unveiling unique properties, thus generating hypotheses that challenge existing paradigms. This perspective injects intriguing complexity into research inquiries. Alternatively, problematization becomes essential when applying a concept like well-being within a context marked by distinctive features. Through problematization, researchers illuminate how the prevailing literature may fall short in addressing the intricacies of the context, thereby presenting opportunities for fresh insights. By highlighting these nuances, researchers can effectively demonstrate how context uniqueness influences understanding the topic at hand, paving the way for novel perspectives.

For instance, in my research on well-being, I explored the concept of agency in the context of Malaysia and the countries in Central America. While I found that human agency is the channel that connects tourism and well-being, the sign of the channel is different when we compare the two cases. In

Central America, human agency moderated this relationship in a negative sense, implying that this region is struggling with satisfying basic needs. Alternatively, the case of Malaysia indicated a positive and significant influence on well-being. The results of these two cases support the distinction that Sen makes between active (Malaysia) and passive (Central America) agency.

Malaysia is a country that is transitioning from developing to developed. Malaysia's microfinance program, Amanah Ikhtiar Malaysia (AIM), aimed at reducing income disparities and empowering women, exemplifies the exercise of agency. Through AIM, individuals, particularly women, have financial resources and opportunities to start or expand their businesses, enhancing their economic agency and contributing to poverty alleviation. Women's increasing participation in the labor force, as evidenced by a rising ratio of female to male labor participation rates, highlights the impact of agency in shaping occupational opportunities and challenging traditional gender roles.

Lesson 10: Limitations Capability Approach and Subjective Well-being

One significant limitation of the capability approach is its emphasis on objective criteria for assessing well-being, which safeguards against emotions and cognitive biases like adaptation. While objectivity is valuable for ensuring consistency and comparability in measuring well-being, it may overlook the subjective dimensions of human experience. In contrast, the paradigm of subjective well-being places a spotlight on feelings, emotions, and personal experiences as central to understanding well-being. This focus acknowledges the inherently subjective nature of human well-being and the importance of subjective perceptions in shaping individuals' overall quality of life. However, relying solely on subjective measures may neglect broader societal factors and structural inequalities that influence well-being outcomes. Thus, while the capability approach offers a comprehensive framework for assessing well-being, its reliance on objective criteria may limit its ability to capture the full range of human experiences. Conversely, subjective well-being provides valuable insights into individuals' emotional states but may benefit from complementary objective measures to provide a more holistic understanding of well-being.

Integrating both perspectives can offer a more nuanced and comprehensive approach to assessing and enhancing overall well-being.

Seven Hypotheses

Based on the provided lessons and research findings, here are clear and cogent hypotheses that can be derived:

Hypothesis 1: Universality of Happiness

- Null Hypothesis (H0): Happiness levels are not consistent across diverse cultural, social, and economic contexts.
- Alternative Hypothesis (H1): Happiness is a universal endeavor transcending cultural, social, and economic boundaries, evidenced by consistent happiness scores across various societies and individuals.

Hypothesis 2: Complex Interplay of Aspirations and Capabilities

- H0: The relationship between aspirations and capabilities is linear and straightforward, with higher aspirations leading to greater happiness if achieved.
- H1: The relationship between aspirations, capabilities, and happiness is nuanced and context-dependent, influenced by structural barriers, socioeconomic constraints, and societal norms, where disparities may lead to feelings of frustration or discontent despite possessing necessary capabilities.

Hypothesis 3: Social Comparison and Happiness

- H0: Social comparison has a consistent impact on happiness across all societal contexts.
- H1: The impact of social comparison on happiness is nuanced and influenced by factors such as development stage, generational

differences, and income distribution within a society, with positive comparisons potentially boosting happiness while disparities may lead to feelings of inadequacy.

Hypothesis 4: Tourism Development and Well-being

- H0: Tourism development has a uniformly positive impact on societal well-being across all regions.
- H1: The relationship between tourism development and well-being is complex, exhibiting threshold effects and nuanced dynamics influenced by factors such as income distribution, source and utilization of tourism-generated income, and contextual peculiarities, requiring adaptive strategies for sustainable growth and equitable distribution of benefits.

Hypothesis 5: Role of Agency and Governance

- H0: Governance plays a dominant role in shaping perceptions of well-being within tourism frameworks across all contexts.
- H1: Human agency is a significant factor influencing the interdependent relationship between tourism and well-being, with governance's influence varying depending on societal structures, institutional efficiency, and political stability.

Hypothesis 6: Contextual Influence on Well-being

- H0: The impact of context on well-being outcomes is negligible, with generalizable findings applicable across diverse contexts.
- H1: Contextual factors significantly influence well-being outcomes, shaping perceptions and experiences differently across regions, necessitating tailored interventions and policy approaches to address unique challenges and opportunities.

Hypothesis 7: Integration of Capability Approach and Subjective Well-being

- H0: The capability approach and subjective well-being offer mutually exclusive perspectives on assessing well-being outcomes.
- H1: Integrating the capability approach and subjective well-being provides a more comprehensive understanding of well-being, leveraging the strengths of both frameworks to capture the objective and subjective dimensions of human experience and societal context.

These hypotheses reflect the complexity and multidimensionality of happiness and well-being in the context of tourism, highlighting the need for nuanced research approaches to explore the intricacies of human flourishing across diverse contexts. See Table 2.

Table 2 The Seven Hypotheses

Hypothesis 1: Universality of Happiness	Null Hypothesis (H0): Happiness levels are not consistent across diverse cultural, social, and economic contexts.	Alternative Hypothesis (H1): Happiness is a universal endeavor transcending cultural, social, and economic boundaries, evidenced by consistent happiness scores across various societies and individuals.
Hypothesis 2: Complex Interplay of Aspirations and Capabilities	H0: The relationship between aspirations and capabilities is linear and straightforward, with higher aspirations leading to greater happiness if achieved.	H1: The relationship between aspirations, capabilities, and happiness is nuanced and context-dependent, influenced by structural barriers, socioeconomic constraints, and societal norms, where disparities may lead to feelings of frustration or discontent despite possessing necessary capabilities.

Hypothesis 3: Social Comparison and Happiness	H0: Social comparison has a consistent impact on happiness across all societal contexts.	H1: The impact of social comparison on happiness is nuanced and influenced by factors such as development stage, generational differences, and income distribution within a society, with positive comparisons potentially boosting happiness while disparities may lead to feelings of inadequacy.
Hypothesis 4: Tourism Development and Well-being	H0: Tourism development has a uniformly positive impact on societal well-being across all regions.	H1: The relationship between tourism development and well-being is complex, exhibiting threshold effects and nuanced dynamics influenced by factors such as income distribution, source and utilization of tourism-generated income, and contextual peculiarities, requiring adaptive strategies for sustainable growth and equitable distribution of benefits.
Hypothesis 5: Role of Agency and Governance	H0: Governance plays a dominant role in shaping perceptions of well-being within tourism frameworks across all contexts.	H1: Human agency is a significant factor influencing the interdependent relationship between tourism and well-being, with governance's influence varying depending on societal structures, institutional efficiency, and political stability.
Hypothesis 6: Contextual Influence on Well-being	H0: The impact of context on well-being outcomes is negligible, with generalizable findings applicable across diverse contexts.	H1: Contextual factors significantly influence well-being outcomes, shaping perceptions and experiences differently across regions, necessitating tailored interventions and policy approaches to address unique challenges and opportunities.
Hypothesis 7: Integration of Capability Approach and Subjective Well-being	H0: The capability approach and subjective well-being offer mutually exclusive perspectives on assessing well-being outcomes.	H1: Integrating the capability approach and subjective well-being provides a more comprehensive understanding of well-being, leveraging the strengths of both frameworks to capture the objective and subjective dimensions of human experience and societal context.

The Path Forward

What can we discern from the insights generated by the capability approach and subjective well-being? Meet Carlos, a lifelong resident of the Caribbean island of Jamaica, who epitomizes the complex relationship residents have with tourism. Carlos thrives as a tour guide, navigating visitors through the island's natural wonders and cultural heritage, benefiting economically from tourism opportunities. Yet, he grapples with the repercussions of tourism's success: overcrowding during peak seasons, strains on infrastructure, and environmental degradation that threatens the landscapes he showcases. Moreover, Carlos observes the erosion of local traditions and identities as commercialization encroaches upon cultural authenticity. His experiences epitomize the delicate balance between reaping economic benefits and preserving the essence of his island home. Carlos's narrative underscores the imperative for sustainable tourism practices that prioritize environmental conservation, community engagement, and cultural integrity to ensure a harmonious coexistence between residents and visitors alike.

Combining the capability approach and subjective well-being in a tourism destination necessitates a comprehensive framework that integrates both objective and subjective dimensions of well-being. Firstly, employing the capability approach involves identifying and assessing the range of capabilities individuals should have access to in the destination, encompassing elements such as education, healthcare, employment, and cultural opportunities. Concurrently, measuring subjective well-being entails capturing residents' feelings, emotions, and overall life satisfaction through surveys or qualitative methods. By integrating objective indicators derived from the capability approach with subjective well-being measures, a nuanced understanding of residents' well-being in the tourism destination can be achieved, highlighting areas where disparities or challenges exist between capabilities and individuals' perceptions of well-being. Moreover, community engagement is pivotal in this process. It empowers residents to voice their concerns and aspirations for well-being enhancement, thus ensuring that tourism development aligns with local needs and preferences.

One approach to integrate these perspectives theoretically is to view subjective well-being as an outcome of individuals' capabilities. That is, the extent to which individuals can achieve their desired levels of happiness and life satisfaction depends on their capabilities. For instance, someone with access to education, healthcare, and employment opportunities may be more likely to report higher subjective well-being than someone lacking these capabilities. Thus, the capability approach provides a framework for understanding the underlying determinants of subjective well-being, emphasizing the role of structural factors, such as social, economic, and environmental conditions, in shaping individuals' well-being outcomes.

Conversely, subjective well-being can also serve as a valuable indicator of the effectiveness of capability expansion efforts. By measuring individuals' subjective experiences and evaluations, researchers and policymakers can assess how capabilities translate into meaningful improvements in people's lives. For example, suppose a community intervention aims to improve access to education. In that case, researchers can evaluate its impact by measuring educational attainment and assessing changes in individuals' subjective well-being, such as their reported levels of happiness and life satisfaction.

In a small island destination like Jamaica, to continue with the example of Carlos, combining the capability approach and subjective well-being theoretically can offer valuable insights into enhancing the well-being of both residents and visitors. First, I would like you to consider the capability approach in action. Imagine a community initiative to improve residents' access to education and vocational training. This initiative expands individuals' capabilities by providing opportunities for skill development and employment, empowering them to pursue meaningful livelihoods and improve their economic well-being. Residents who previously lacked access to education or training can now secure stable jobs in the tourism industry, contributing to their sense of agency and self-determination.

Next, look at how subjective well-being can complement this approach. Researchers could conduct surveys or interviews with residents to assess their levels of happiness, life satisfaction, and overall well-being before and after the implementation of the education and training initiative. By capturing residents' subjective experiences and evaluations, researchers can gauge the impact of the capability expansion efforts on their well-being outcomes. For example, residents who have benefited from the initiative may report higher happiness and life satisfaction levels than those who have not participated, indicating that the program has effectively translated capabilities into improved subjective well-being.

Integrating the capability approach alongside subjective well-being offers valuable insights for informing tourism development strategies in Jamaica. For example, policymakers can prioritize initiatives to enhance residents' capabilities, such as improving access to education, healthcare, and economic opportunities. Additionally, policymakers should consider residents' subjective well-being by actively engaging with them to understand their feelings, emotions, and experiences. By assessing residents' aspirations and expectations, as well as the realities they face, policymakers can identify potential gaps between what individuals desire and what they experience. This gap between aspirations and reality can serve as a crucial dependent variable influenced by various factors, including individuals' agency and the acquisition of resources. Through a causal sequence of events, these resources translate into functionings that, when valued as capabilities, contribute to overall well-being and agency goals, ultimately leading to a higher quality of life. It is critical to recognize that this process is non-linear and influenced by evolving personal, social, and environmental factors. By considering objective capabilities and subjective well-being, policymakers can develop more holistic and effective tourism development strategies that prioritize the well-being of Jamaica's residents.

Final Words

Standing at this crossroads, I am filled with both culmination and anticipation. The conclusion of this chapter marks not an end but a new beginning — a launchpad for further exploration and theoretical discovery. Armed with the wisdom accrued through my research endeavors, I am poised to chart a course toward uncharted territories of knowledge. I envision a future brimming with possibility and potential in the chapters yet to be written. My journey does not conclude here; it extends into endless inquiry and innovation. With each step forward, I will continue to push the boundaries of knowledge, unravel the mysteries that lie beyond, and contribute meaningfully to the collective tapestry of human understanding.

Thus, as I bid farewell to this chapter of my research expedition, I do so with gratitude for the experiences it has bestowed upon me and a fervent commitment to the journey ahead. For in the pursuit of knowledge, there is no final destination, only an ever-unfolding horizon of discovery and wonder.

Selected own references

Croes, R., Shapoval, V., Rivera, M., Bak, M. & Zientara, P. (2024). Promoting Residents' Happiness Through a Human-Centric Approach to Tourism City Development. *International Journal of Tourism Cities*, https://doi.org/10.1108/IJTC-05-2023-0105.

Croes, R., Kubickova, M., & Ridderstaat, J. (2023). Destination Competitiveness and Human Development: The Compelling Critical Force of Human Agency. *Journal of Hospitality & Tourism Research*, 47(4), 62-75. https://doi.org/10.1177/10963480221140022.

Croes, R., Ridderstaat, J., Bak, M. & Zientara, P. (2021). Tourism specialization, economic growth, human development, and transition economies: the case of Poland. *Tourism Management*, 82, 104181.

Croes, R., Ridderstaat, J. & Shapoval, V. (2020). Connecting tourism competitiveness to human development. *Annals of Tourism Research*, 80, January (102825).

Croes, R., Van Niekerk, M., & Ridderstaat, J. (2018). Tourism specialization and quality of life: Evidence from Malta. *Tourism Management*, 68, 212-223.

Kubickova, M., Croes, R., & Rivera, M. (2017). Human agency shaping tourism competitiveness and quality of life. *Tourism Management Perspective*, 22, 120-131.

Croes, R. & Rivera, M. (2017). Tourism potential to benefit the poor: A social accounting matrix model applied to Ecuador. *Tourism Economics*, 23(1), 29-48.

Rivera, M., Croes, R., & Lee, S. (2016). Tourism development and happiness: A residents' perspective. *Journal of Destination Marketing & Management*, 5(1), 5-15.

Ridderstaat, J., Croes, R., & Nijkamp, P. (2016). The tourism development-quality of life nexus in a small island destination. *Journal of Travel Research*, 55(1), 79-94.

Ridderstaat, J., Croes, R., & Nijkamp, P. (2016). A two-way causal chain between tourism development and quality of life in a small island destination: An empirical analysis. *Journal of Sustainable Tourism*, 24 (10), 1461-1479.

Croes, R. (2012). Assessing tourism development from Sen's capability approach. *Journal of Travel Research*, 51(5), 542-554.

Croes, R. (2022). *Small Island and small destination tourism. Overcoming the smallness barrier for economic growth and tourism competitiveness.* Apple Academic Press: Waretown, NJ, USA.

Croes, R. & Rivera, M. (2016). *Poverty Alleviation through Tourism Development: A Comprehensive and Integrated Approach.* Apple Academic Press: Waretown, NJ, USA.

Croes, R. & Yang, Y. (2022). (eds.) *A modern guide to tourism economics.* Edward Elgar Publishing: Cheltenham, UK.

Croes, R., Rivera, M., & Semrad, K. (2018). Subjective well-being and tourism development in small island destinations. In McLeod, M. & Croes, R. *Tourism Management in Warm-water Island Destinations.* CABI: Wallingford, UK.

Croes, R. (2012). Tourism, poverty relief, and the quality-of-life in developing countries. In Uysal, M., Perdue, R. & Sirgy, J. (eds.) *Handbook of Tourism and Quality-of-Life Research: Enhancing the Lives of Tourists and Residents of Host Communities*, Springer Publishers, Dordrecht, The Netherlands.

Brief biography of Dr. Robertico Croes

Dr. Robertico Croes, an esteemed professor at UCF Rosen College of Hospitality Management, is renowned for his expertise in tourism economics and management, with a focus on advancing human development in economically constrained regions. Serving as Editor for the Rosen Research Review, he's authored six books, including "Small Island and Small Destination Tourism" and "A Modern Guide to Tourism Economics," alongside over 100 publications and contributions to numerous books and industry reports. Notably, his work has earned him a spot among the top 2% cited authors by Stanford University.

Dr. Croes' impact extends beyond academia. He co-authored a pivotal report on coastal and marine tourism sustainability presented at the United Nations Ocean Conference. His leadership of the Infectious Disease and Travel Health Project, backed by significant funding, underscores his commitment to addressing contemporary challenges.

His tenure at UCF Rosen College showcases versatile leadership roles, from directing the Dick Pope Sr. Institute for Tourism Studies to serving as Associate Dean and department chair. His expertise spans econometrics in hospitality, tourism demand analysis, and assessing tourism's economic impact, particularly in fostering sustainable development and poverty alleviation.

Dr. Croes' global influence is evident through presentations in numerous countries and prestigious conferences worldwide. Recently, he was invited by the President of the United Nations General Assembly to participate as a speaker in the High-Level Thematic Event on Tourism, as part of the first-ever United Nations General Assembly Sustainability Week, at the UN Headquarters, New York.

He has also provided consultation services internationally, contributing to tourism master plans and strategic advisement in various nations.

With a funding track record exceeding $14 million and numerous accolades, including research awards and editorial board positions, Dr. Croes is a beacon in his field. His career trajectory, from governmental roles in Aruba to academia, reflects a commitment to public service and scholarly excellence. His values shine through his dedication to mentorship and knowledge sharing, leaving an indelible mark on both academia and policy, positively impacting communities worldwide.

https://hospitality.ucf.edu/person/robertico-croes/

www.ingramcontent.com/pod-product-compliance
Lightning Source LLC
Chambersburg PA
CBHW021408210526
45463CB00001B/267